ZEN
ON THE GO

A DRAWING TOGETHER OF SIMPLE YET DEEP LIFE EXPERIENCES.

ADITI PANT

Notion Press

Old No. 38, New No. 6
McNichols Road, Chetpet
Chennai - 600 031

First Published by Notion Press 2019
Copyright © Aditi Pant 2019
All Rights Reserved.

ISBN 978-1-64650-591-3

This book has been published with all efforts taken to make the material error-free after the consent of the author. However, the author and the publisher do not assume and hereby disclaim any liability to any party for any loss, damage, or disruption caused by errors or omissions, whether such errors or omissions result from negligence, accident, or any other cause.

While every effort has been made to avoid any mistake or omission, this publication is being sold on the condition and understanding that neither the author nor the publishers or printers would be liable in any manner to any person by reason of any mistake or omission in this publication or for any action taken or omitted to be taken or advice rendered or accepted on the basis of this work. For any defect in printing or binding the publishers will be liable only to replace the defective copy by another copy of this work then available.

Dedication

This book is dedicated to my daughters Akshi and Aishi who are a constant source of pride, joy and inspiration.

Contents

Acknowledgements 11

Zen on the Go 13

1. A Beginning 15

2. A Storm in a Teacup 18

3. A Blast from the Past 21

4. A Deity in Jeans and T-shirt 24

5. A Leader is Also a Dealer in Humor 26

6. A Lesson in Humility 29

7. A Moment of Magic 32

8. Actions Do Speak Louder Than Words 35

9. Around the World in Less Than a Minute 38

10. Be True to Yourself 41

11. Calm is Super Power 43

12. Connecting with the Roots 46

13. Creativity at Work. 49

14. Dancing with the Wind 52

15. Finding Extraordinary in the Ordinary 55

16. Follow Your Heart: It Knows the Way. 58

17. It is in Giving That We Receive. 61

18. A Chance at Living Many Lives. 64

19. From a Child's Mouth. 68

20. Happily Married? 71

21. Home is Where You Find It 74

22. Insight 77

23. Don't Miss the Signs 80

24. Journey Into Yourself. 83

25. Kindness of a Stranger. 86

26. Labour of Love 89

27. Lemon Tree. 92

28. Let It Go 95

29. Let Love In 98

30. Giving Meaning to Your Life. 101

31. Let There Be Light .104

32. Life Begins at the End of Your Comfort Zone . . .107

33. Life is a Lesson in Humility. 110

34. Life is But a Game...........................112

35. Life Lessons from Daughters..................115

36. Mind Over Matter 118

37. Miracles Grow Where You Plant Them 121

38. Music...the Voice of the Soul 123

39. Natural Order 126

40. From Nature's Laboratory 129

41. Of Birds and Butterflies.....................132

42. On Learning 135

43. Life Teaches You When You Are Mindful 138

44. Paper Boats 142

45. Parenting – Means Growing with
    Your Children 145

46. Paved Paradise............................148

47. Pay It Forward.............................151

48. Angel with Fur Instead of Wings.............154

49. Pura Vida! 157

50. Question the Question 160

51. Seeing Beyond Exteriors 163

52. Simple Living 166

53. Simple Yet Significant 169

54. Stairway to Heaven 172

55. Stop Reacting. Start Responding 175

56. Take Care of Yourself. .178

57. The Art of Gifting. 181

58. The Art of Giving 184

59. The Avengers! 187

60. The Best Journey Takes You Home 190

61. God's Plan. 192

62. The Bigger Picture 195

63. The 'C' Word 198

64. The Greatest Challenge. 201

65. The Juggler 204

66. The Land of the Gods. .207

67. The Salt of the Earth. 210

68. The Secret Ingredient 213

69. The Seeker and the Sought 216

70. The Sheltering Tree. 218

71. The Voice That Doesn't Use Words 221

72. Travel Light, Travel Free 224

73. Treasure Hunt. 226

74. Welcome to the Jungle .229

75. What Goes Around Comes Around 232

76. Where Dandelions Grow.................234

77. Well Done is Better Than Well Said 237

78. You Can Only Conquer Yourself............240

79. Zen on the Go 243

Acknowledgements

First and foremost I would like to thank my father Mahanand Paliwal. In the process of putting this book together I realized how true this gift of writing is for me. You have given me both; the wings to pursue my dreams and the roots to follow my passion home.

To my mother, Basanti Paliwal. Despite toying with words all the time, I can barely find the right words to express all the wisdom, love and support you've given me.

To my husband, Atul Pant, thank you for all the deliberations on Osho, Sadhguru and life in general. All the good that comes from this book and from life I look forward to sharing with you.

To my friend Pritam Benjamin, my father in law, Kailash Chandra and my sister Richa Satyawali; for patiently reading all the articles and enthusing me with your support and encouragement.

To my family, friends and colleagues, you have all been a vital part of my journey. Thank you!

To Deccan Herald for publishing all my articles on a regular basis. Thinking about what I am going to write next and reflecting on what I wrote was a life changing experience.

Last but not the least my publishers at notion press- you gave life to my manuscript.

Zen on the Go

If truth is what you seek, then the examined life will take you on a long ride to the limits of solitude and leave you by the side of the road with your truth and nothing else."

– Thomas Ligotti

On that very side of the road I learnt that stories matter. The esoteric becomes real in the telling and retelling of stories. In a world that seems to be spinning in different directions a story/anecdote provides a pause; a quick moment of tranquility, of reflection, before we jump into the fray again. The stories we love do live in us forever and in the little episodes we might find fragments of ourselves or of our lives and also a way to put it all together. Little stories often give us the big picture and tell us what we must hold on to and what we must let go. They surprise us, they make us think and feel and teach us how to quieten our own disquiets. They take us back to those simple things, those glorious things, those things so often forgotten but so desperately needed.

In this collection I've used stories and anecdotes to entreat the heart and the mind. Some of these anecdotal experiences are mine and some are borrowed from the experiences of others or from stories I've read or heard. We do not learn just by our experiences, but rather by reflecting on those experiences. The little stories underscore the importance of personal experiences, everyday happenings and seemingly trivial things that come up in our lives or in retrospect and how such big wisdom can be found in such little things!

These articles and the tiny stories in them underline the fact that reflection changes an ordinary experience into something extraordinary. They elucidate how by examining our own life we make it meaningful and enduring. This is the reason why storytellers never pass on…they just escape into their own story.

- 1 -

A Beginning...

For months at a time my father would be away from home. His work necessitated transfers and travels and we got used to his sporadic visits during our childhood years. Of course we missed him, however, he made the time he was at home so meaningful and memorable that despite him not being around his presence ricocheted within the walls of our home.

One aspect that went a long way in underscoring his presence in the house was the distinctive way he addressed our childhood delinquencies and concerns. He could have easily 'sorted us out' by chastisements and penalties …but he didn't. Instead he would tell us a story.

Almost every night, he would gather the three of us around him and tell us stories from all walks of life. The epics Ramayana and Mahabharatha got copious episodic mentions. He would use these stories to teach us a lesson and more often than not it worked.

Once when he saw one of us getting too conceited with our successes he told us the story of Bhima from the Mahabharatha; Bhima was mighty and powerful. At some point his strength and sway made him too proud. Once he came across a monkey sleeping in his path. At first he made a sound to scare the monkey away, however the monkey did not dislodge from his comfortable position. Bhima then ordered the monkey to get out of his way. The monkey humbly said, "I am too old and weak to move. Do push my tail aside to make way for yourself." Bhima scoffed at the monkey and then tried to move its tail …but in vain. As the powerful Bhima failed again and again at moving the monkey's tail, it suddenly dawned on him that he was in the presence of a mystical being. When he bowed down in repentance, the monkey revealed its true form. Seeing lord Hanuman in place of the monkey, Bhima was truly humbled.

After telling the story my father left us to make our own deductions. The stories were so pointed that they seldom failed to leave a mark. We understood the implicit and sometimes the not so implicit message and went to bed contemplative yet revived. His story telling was a huge part of my childhood and even now I marvel at his ingenious way of correcting and guiding us despite the paucity of time he had with us during our formative years.

It is no wonder that I have come to believe that telling stories is an effective way of building the moral fiber. Every anecdote/story in his book stems from what I learnt as a child and also what I continue to learn every day. There isn't a stronger connection between people than storytelling. Stories you hear and tell make you what you are. We build ourselves out of those stories.

– 2 –

A Storm in a Teacup

When they say God is in the details, they simply mean that if we look closely and long enough we will find everything we need to know about life and living in the ordinary quotidian occurrences. Given a chance, it is the commonplace, small things that can lend perpetuity to a moment.

Take your daily cup of tea for instance. It can sometimes become a panacea for a bad day, balm for pain, manna for the tired and even a celebration for a day well spent. There is something about the nature of tea that nurtures quiet contemplation and lenient relaxation. And sometimes you may even find jewels in terms of wisdom at the bottom of your cup.

To unwind after a particularly tiring day I sat with my cup of tea and a book under the dappled shade of a tree in my lawn. I looked forward to the best time of my day. I opened my book, looked around at the verdant landscape and took a sip of tea. The magic evaporated. I had forgotten to put sugar in my tea.

I was too languid, too much in sync with my surroundings to disturb the tranquility and get sugar for my tea. I somehow struggled with my cup till I reached the lees and discovered undissolved sugar crystals at the bottom. By then it was already too late.

Life is unpredictable, and even your finest moments could be laced with irony and or disappointment. Best laid plans can be thwarted, because you either forgot to add sugar, were too lazy to get sugar, or too preoccupied to notice the sugar crystals at the bottom of your cup. You have two options when life throws such curve balls at you. Either you fret and remain disenchanted over something you can't control or you laugh at your own inanity and at life's ability to surprise you at every turn. A sense of humour goes a long way in helping you overlook the ugly truths that surface suddenly. It gives you the best armor against the unexpected and helps you find your bearings when everything else seems to be crumbling. Go after life just like it comes after you.

I got up from my sanctuary, chuckled, shook my head and went inside to make another cup of tea.

– 3 –

A Blast from the Past

Ever wondered what makes old things so wonderful and sweet? Recently, someone in my extended family celebrated their 25th wedding anniversary. The theme for the party was 'retro'. Everyone was excited as they pondered over dresses, hairstyles, music and effects of the days gone by. It seemed the entire family came together discussing their experience of an analogous past replete with nostalgic moments.

It is said "the good old days" are a myth. No one ever considered they were good at the time. Every age has consisted of trials and tribulations that seemed insufferable to the people who lived through them. Despite this Owens Lee Pomeroy says "Nostalgia is like a grammar lesson: you find the present tense, but the past perfect!" I am intrigued. Why is the past concomitant with such fondness, regard and romance?

One can only speculate. We are told to revel in our present and we often obsess about our future, however, the present is unfolding as we speak and the future looms unknown. To add to this our 'now' is often riddled with complexities and stresses that we fathom and work out as we move along. With every passing day the change in trends, norms, demographics, environments and psyche point towards a future that we cannot even conceive today. In this mayhem and constant endeavour to make sense of our today and tomorrow, one absolute certainty is our yesterday. There are no upheavals there; it's already been and done. God may possibly work upon and change our present or future but even God can't change our past. That is something we will always have, safe in our memory and experiences that have shaped us and made us who we are today.

The hectic pace of our lives ensures that we do not stay in the past for long. We have obligations to fulfil, dreams that need to be actualized and deadlines to meet. Despite this our past will still find us when we least expect it to. It beats inside us like a second heart. A long forgotten lullaby will bring nostalgic tears to our eyes. A particular aroma in an unknown terrain might transport us back home. A forgotten flower/note in a book could bring a poignant smile to our face. Our hearts will beat a little faster as we tread the familiar road to our childhood home. A photo album time and again becomes our solace and a delightful way to pass time. Only in the past delayed gratification is romantic instead of exasperating. All this happens simply because everything we experience becomes a part of us and all these little scattered parts of us connect to make a whole. Our sojourn to the past leaves us rejuvenated, consoled, warmed and enthused.

It comes as no surprise then that the 'retro' party was a huge success where everyone got a chance to relive their past. It was amidst laughter, surprise, awe and reminiscing that I came to the conclusion that it doesn't matter whether the 'good old days' were really good. What matters is our belief that they were.

– 4 –

A Deity in Jeans and T-shirt

In one of his discourses Osho narrated the story of a Zen philosopher who was sitting on the 10th floor of a restaurant in Japan, having dinner with a friend when suddenly an earthquake struck. In seconds there was chaos as people tried to find shelter and protection. The staircases were jammed, fear was palpable and shrieks and commotion pervaded the air. As the friend of the Zen philosopher ran towards the stairs he noticed his dinner companion sitting calmly. If anything, he had made himself more comfortable. His eyes were closed as if in meditation. The philosopher's friend did not have the heart to run after witnessing this unusual sight in the midst of all the pandemonium. He went to his friend "Why are you still sitting here? Let's run" he urged. The philosopher opened his eyes and said; "We are in the 10th floor…where can we go? The earthquake is in the 9th floor, in the 8th floor and in every other floor of this building. It's even outside this building. If I must run I will run to the only place where this earthquake cannot touch me. That place is deep within me…not outside. So, I'm running inward just as everyone else is running outside."

When facing a problem, we almost always seek help, run outwards to fix it, not realising that the solutions we seek are often inside us. The world is a loud noisy place and other people's voices often pour in and drown out your words. All we need to do is find silence, open a gap for the voice within, create a space and be patient. At our deepest level, within our soul, we are created in God's image. There is a deity inside who speaks to us so clearly that we need no other assurance. It is ironical how it's hard for us to believe in our inner strength, in our own profundity and yet we believe in abstract notions such as love and sorrow. It is the divine light within us that lights up the universe and once we understand this; understand that the world is only an extension of who we are inside - no earthquake can shake our state of equilibrium.

- 5 -

A Leader is Also a Dealer in Humor

Leadership is hard to define, and more often than not good leadership is a series of simple gracious acts rather than a single act of bravado or brilliance. What I have come to realize is that when you make people feel comfortable and guide them to the cradle of their own power then you empower happy employees who characterize what you want to see in an organization. A sense of humor goes a long way in fostering that feeling of comfort and ease.

Humor can positively amend any situation and help us cope at the very instant we begin laughing. Through humor, one can soften the blow of some difficult circumstances that life might throw at us. Minutes before giving my first address as the Vice Principal of the school I was edgy. Of course I was ready, and knew what I was going to speak was crisp and meaningful, yet the butterflies in my stomach were fast changing to dragonflies. I had written my speech down on a piece of paper and clenched it as though my life depended upon it. I sat among the dignitaries outwardly poised while everything churned on the inside.

The function began with the lighting of the lamp. This was the first time I was to be a part of this solemn occasion. In my disconcerted state I didn't realize that while lighting the wick I had actually put to flame the piece of paper in my hand. My speech! Mrs. Rao, the Principal of the school noticed the flames first and nudged me. Before others could catch a glimpse I quickly put the little fire out. My first speech as the Vice Principal now rested on half burnt crumpled paper.

I thought this entire episode would make the Principal rather upset; instead she just laughed. "Aditi, I've done sillier and funnier things than this when I first became Principal and still continue to do so" she said with a twinkle in her eye as I sat next to her mortified. "Don't worry about it, inane things happen to the best of us. Just see the humor in it dear". I'm not sure if such fiascos were ever a part of her life as she is a rather composed individual. I'm sure she said what she did just to put me at ease and make me see that mistakes and viewing them with equanimity is all in a day's work. I felt relaxed. In fact, I chuckled to myself.

When the time came I gave my speech with some aplomb. As I basked in the applause, I realized that no matter how trying the circumstances, it is one's response or reaction that counts. And if that response is tempered with humor like that of Ms. Rao, it repairs, reassures and rebuilds our belief in all that is good in this world. A good leader exemplifies that mistakes are a part of life and should be dealt with amusement and equanimity.

Like a welcome summer rain, effective leadership with a healthy mix of humor may suddenly cleanse and cool the earth, the air and you.

- 6 -

A Lesson in Humility

We are mere tools; it is God who does all the work. The fact that God works through us is not a reward or an accomplishment, it's a gift that is bestowed upon us without asking.

During the great 'Mahabharatha' the battle between Arjun and Karna was intense. With Arjun's incessant arrows the chariot of Karna would go 20-25 paces behind and despite Karna's determined aims Arjun's chariot would go only 2-3 paces behind. Yet each time this happened, Lord Krishna who was charioting Arjun's chariot loudly praised Karna's skill in archery and overlooked Arjun's more obvious manoeuvres. Arjun tried to take it all in his stride, but, when this happened repeatedly he felt compelled to speak. "My powerful archery is moving Karna's chariot more than 20 paces behind and his arrows are only moving my chariot by one or two paces, yet you praise his skill and disregard mine" he said with some discontent. "How is he better than me? Am I not more powerful?" he questioned.

With a sagacious smile Krishna responded. "You have the massive Hanuman in your flag, the mighty Shesh Naag at your wheels and the Lord himself as the charioteer. Despite this divine intervention if Karna is still able to move your chariot by a few paces …can you imagine the extent of his skill at Archery? I cannot help but praise him."

It is said that when the war got over and Lord Krishna came down from the chariot, it went up in flames. The chariot was already destroyed by the arrows of Karna, it is only the presence of God that was holding it up together. It is also said this that when Arjun heard and saw this, his eyes filled up with repentant tears. His pride and arrogance disintegrated and he fell at the feet of Lord Krishna. He realised that he was only as powerful as the Lord who was protecting him.

There is a lesson in this tryst with mythology. Without the blessing of God, we can accomplish nothing. We need to be humble as we are mere instruments he uses to write with. He is the creator and author, we can only appreciate his penmanship and craft and be gratified that he decided to use us in his story.

- 7 -

A Moment of Magic

The mysteries of the universe flow in us like a river and those of us who no longer pause to wonder, to drink, to bathe in this ephemeral river fail to gain insight into the mystery of life. Caught in the mundane, our faculties are so dulled that they cannot comprehend that utmost wisdom and radiant beauty lies in realizing that the incredible becomes real when we begin to recognize the magic in our own lives.

Looking for a way to spend an idyllic afternoon, I happened to watch a movie called 'forever my girl'. The movie was nothing out of the ordinary however, it did have moving scenes and leisurely pace that lulled the heart. In one poignant moment the protagonist, who is a guitarist and also a singer incidentally realizes that his daughter (who he didn't know about) shows natural affinity towards playing a guitar. Even though she has never learnt or played the instrument before she is able to replicate exactly what her father had played for her a few minutes ago. He is overwhelmed by the revelation and enchantment of the moment.There was nothing earth shattering in the scene, however, it did spread a certain warmth and joy.

My husband a chemical engineer and a scientist is naturally drawn to the mysteries of the chemical amalgamations and transformations. My daughter who could choose to write a research paper in any one out of the 7 subjects she was studying for high school, chose chemistry. Her natural affinity towards the subject is a given and we've never thought to ponder upon it. What is interesting however, is the fact that while I was watching the movie about the guitarist father and daughter, right in my own home in another room my husband and my daughter were discussing her proposal for writing the paper in chemistry. How was it that I could recognize this poignancy of the moment in the movie and not in my own home? How is it that little revelations, little miracles, little wonders occur to us every day and yet we fail to notice them? It takes an external medium to bring the message home to us.

Once our sense perception grows stronger, and we become more mindful, we will be able to see the magic in little things. The consistent mark of wisdom is to see the miraculous in what is seemingly common.

– 8 –

Actions Do Speak Louder Than Words

Our life is not a representation of the thoughts we hold in our mind or the words we speak but rather a replication of the actions we do-both big and small. Hence, what you think and say might not be as significant as what you do.

My younger daughter Aishi is particularly concerned about carbon footprints in general and her own in particular. She advocates saving the natural resources and continuously reminds us at home to be careful regarding how we spend this precious commodity in our day to day lives. We indulge her …never really taking her seriously. At one point, however, it was her seemingly miniscule action that made me appreciate the fact that actions, albeit small, can be powerful.

Circumstances necessitated that we move to a temporary accommodation for a while. In one corner of the house the water would drip faintly from one of the taps despite being tightly wound. Since the trickle was nominal we didn't bother much with it and got on with more important tasks. After a few days I noticed my daughter taking a mug of water out every day to water the potted plants. Busy with morning chores, I never gave it much thought. She did this for almost a month before I finally took notice. I realized then, she would place the mug below the leaking tap every night and every morning when the mug was almost full she would use it to water the plants. She would repeat the process in the morning and again water the plants in the evening. Rather self-consciously I acknowledge; she did this without being told, without telling anyone and without waiting for the 'adults' to take any action. My entire family and the healthy potted plants came to appreciate the fact that she was genuinely concerned about the environment.

Coming back to the main issue, people may have misgivings about what you say but they will certainly believe what you do. Just like seeds in an infertile land all your good intentions and thoughts will amount to nothing, unless actions like rain and sunshine bring them to fruition. When you put your heart, mind and soul into the smallest acts, you leave footprints of kindness wherever you go.

– 9 –

Around the World in Less Than a Minute

Indian mythology is replete with stories that never fail to enlighten the mind and touch the heart. The simplicity yet craft in this one makes it particularly poignant.

Narada once presented Lord Shiva with an extraordinary Mango given to him by Lord Brahma. Anyone, who ate this mango would be blessed with great knowledge and wisdom. Being a father of two sons Lord Shiva resolved his dilemma by consulting his wife Parvati. They decided give the mango to the son who won a race designed by them.

The competition involved the two circling the world three times. Whoever could do it first would get the precious mango. The competition seemed fair enough, however, Ganesha was in a predicament. His mode of transport was a mouse and his brother's a peacock which was more agile and fast. Secondly, Ganesha was rather plump and his brother not only fit but also a go getter. While Ganesha was still contemplating Kartikeya was already well on his way. At some point Kartikeya did feel like Ganesha was ahead of him but smiling at the inanity of the idea he charged ahead.

After deep thought, Ganesha asked his parents to sit together. He then joined his hands together as if in prayer and walked around them thrice. Lord Shiva smiled but Goddess Parvati looked baffled as Ganesha now asked them for the Mango.

"But you haven't even circled the world once, leave alone thrice" argued Parvati.

Ganesha smiled sagaciously as he replied, "You are my entire world; my world is only an extension of both of you. Circling you thrice meant circling the world thrice". All arguments died. Ganesha got the Mango.

At the surface of it the story seems to underscore the power of wit, however at a deeper level it talks about how our beliefs and innate wisdom can compass our thoughts in the right direction. Ganesha's spirit of love and reverence for his parents gave him a perspective that can only be attained when you let go of the notions created by the world around you and look for answers within. If kartikeya had paused for a minute, sought meaning in what he was attempting to do, maybe his 'world view' would have changed.

– 10 –

Be True to Yourself

Often in perusing short term benefits and goals we go against our natural state not realizing that in the long run it will rob us of our innate power and happiness. True joy is actualized when you are truly yourself. The lion is said to be the king of the jungle. The same lion can be in a zoo or in the circus. In the zoo the lion's basic requirements are met and he could be content. In a circus he is the center of attraction and gets the adulation of most. But in both the cases he is removed from his elements. Only in the jungle can we see a Lion's true disposition; and when the lion is himself he powerful. He is the king.

My daughter was recently chosen to be the master of the ceremony in a school event. Emceeing the annual event in school is an honorable and coveted task. My daughter was not immune to the charm of the popular role and auditioned for it attentively. During the rehearsals, she did an amazing job and everyone not only spoke highly of her eloquence but also thought she was perfect for the job. Akshi did her job diligently but her heart was in singing for the choir. Being the host for the evening gave her a high but singing gave her true delight. Since in singing she felt she was most herself she decided to follow her heart.

She hosted the program for the first half of the event and then joined the choir towards the latter half. This way she not only gave someone else a chance at emceeing the event but also did what came most naturally to her. When I saw her sing to her heart's content during the annual day program I knew that she was truly happy. Not all of us can resolve our predicament this easily, however, all of us can and must make a brave attempt to be true to ourselves. This way we embrace our uniqueness; our destiny.

The moon sticks to its course, stays faithful to its true nature. This is perhaps why it has the power to pull an entire ocean from shore to shore and the beauty to leave everyone mesmerized.

– 11 –

Calm is Super Power

A n old fable from the animal kingdom goes like this. In a moment of misplaced gumption, a donkey, drunk on false pride and arrogance challenged a lion to a duel. The lion listened to the donkey and quietly walked away. The donkey was jubilant and took this as a sign of victory. This deeply disturbed a fox who witnessed this unusual scene. Known for its cunning, and curiosity the fox soon approached the lion to coax a response out of him.

"How could you walk away from a situation like this? Have you forgotten that you are a Lion…the king of the Jungle? How could you be so timid in the face of such a juvenile threat posed by the donkey?

The Lion equivocated; "Look closely …the answer my dear friend lies in the heart of your question".

The fox thought for a moment but could not resolve this puzzle. "Stop speaking in riddles. Why did you walk away?"

Almost reluctantly the lion answered. "You just stated that I am the king of the jungle and that the donkey's challenge was juvenile. The best response in such a situation was to walk away silently. I could kill the donkey effortlessly but that would mean I had accepted his challenge. Accepting his challenge would put me in the same plane as the donkey. It would mitigate my sagacity, station and wisdom. Therefore, I decided to walk away wordlessly. Ignoring the donkey's oblivious remark was the best resolution to maintain my state of calm and balance."

The fox bowed down to the king of the jungle and retreated silently.

Often, life greets us with petty remarks and people. Like the lion we always have two options. Either to retaliate and react, which not only makes the situation murky but also takes you away from your state of equilibrium. The other option, let's say the lion's option is to distance yourself from the situation. You ignore such remarks and people and continue on your journey without a dent in your esteem, composure and sense of balance.

Silence is power. Calm is super power. Exercise them.

- 12 -

Connecting with the Roots

"Maybe you are searching among the branches, for what only appears in the roots."

– Rumi

We never really leave a place, we carry it within us in our memories and in anecdotal stories of where we have been and what we have experienced. Many such stories are told and retold when my in-laws are visiting us. My Father in Law was in the Indian Army and his work mandated that every few years the family move to a new location. They made a home only to move again in a few years. Despite the transfer always being a daunting task, they accepted it gracefully and had become deft at establishing quick roots. My father in law's mother, took her kitchen garden in her mind's eye wherever she went. Blessed with a green thumb she would plant a garden and grow all kinds of plants; this would go a long way in establishing 'a home', despite the constant movement and disruption. By association, my mother in law learnt about the nuances of gardening (kitchen or otherwise) and the art of moving on. And again, by association I learnt my own lesson about letting go through an interesting experience.

Spring was in full swing and Bangalore a riot of colour and blossom. My own little garden was a pictorial joy. Nascent greens, pinks and reds were fighting for space and attention. It was a true pleasure to bask in this beauty after a hard day's toil. However, I came back from work one day to a disturbing sight. All the beautiful plants had been chopped off, and the stumps glared back at me. I was confused, angry and upset.

"Why would anyone cut them off"? I asked no one in particular. My Mother in law answered. "The roots have been ignored for a while now. They also need nourishment. This is the best time to prune the plants as, the natural fecundity during spring will make the plants grow back again faster. The flowers and plants will be much stronger as in clipping them the consideration has gone to the roots". I knew she was speaking from experience.

The insight disseminated by my husband's grandmother found its way to me through his mother's words. Albeit Reluctantly, I learnt my lesson that no matter how difficult, it is important to let go. To start something new and fresh one must readdress the old; the roots. Discomfort and anguish are the bedrock of strength and courage and only the tenacity, patience and wisdom of nature can teach us that. Hence in all the stories that are told and retold in the household, I added one of my own. This spring the sunshine in the rain and the rain in the sunshine elucidated that pain and happiness mingle in life and that while the branches might help you touch the sky; the roots will take you home.

– 13 –

Creativity at Work

At work and otherwise, so caught up are we in the mundane that creativity and innovative thinking often eludes us. Our CEO and mentor often gives us creative confidence tasks that require us to come up with creative solutions. He believes that as educators we are in the business of creativity, and that one inspired idea will not do; we need to have many creative ideas and then some more. He hopes that once the domino effect materialises the resultant will be seamless and enterprising.

We are rather poor students most of the time, however, he never quite gives up on us. Once, in an attempt to make us more enterprising he gave us the task of writing our own obituary. After we got over the morbid implications of the entire notion, and began our task, we realised we had nothing special to write about. Each day melted into another and in meeting the demands of the day and time we had left our aspirations far behind. Ready or not we were enforced to revisit our childhood dreams, take a deep look at our present and envision our future with more focus and clarity.

One of the primal needs of man is to leave behind a legacy. To be remembered and to be remembered well. While working towards the requirements of the task, we were obligated to take a good look at ourselves. We also realised that if we didn't like what we saw, we had the power to change that. It didn't matter whether we completed writing our obituary, what mattered, however, was the fact that each one of us started thinking about our professional and personal goals.

The ability to think originally, question the herd, imagine new scenarios, and produce astonishing work is the demand of the time and to be able to do this one must be creative. Dissonance and then deconstruction of ideas and notions that hold one back is the first step and hence at some point ingenuity could look like destruction. Let it happen. Let it all crumble to dust before it emerges with a new shape and dimension.

When the image we had of ourselves crumbled we were able to salvage our true form. In the process we learnt to think about our legacy and realised we were writing it every day.

– 14 –

Dancing with the Wind

Just a few days ago Bangalore was gripped by a sudden thunderstorm. Even as storms go, this one was particularly violent. The temperamental winds were relentless and the lightning and thunder only underscored the power that nature can wield over man. Trees were either torn or completely uprooted. Even the sturdy electric poles were dislodged. The destruction was only too evident the next day as we drove to school. My younger daughter, who displays a deep affinity towards nature was very perturbed. She however, also noted that certain trees did not seem ravaged by the storm. She asked her father, "Papa, why is it that certain trees are completely displaced and others are not even touched by the storm". I could make out that she had been eavesdropping on some of our previous conversations when she asked her second question. "What about karma?" she asked. I was taken aback by the turn this conversation had taken and gave a quick response. "The law of Karma doesn't apply to nature". As suspected, this response did not impress her and she looked even more confused.

As I contemplated upon how to best address this question my husband came up with a well thought of response. "The trees that were weak and did not bend with the wind were wrecked. The trees that were resilient and danced with the wind did not break. They could withstand the ravages of the storm". This answer appealed to her child like sensibility and she continued to stare at the disrupted landscape.

There is a message for us adults too in this ordinary incident. More often than not we try to control things that are beyond us. We resist, contest and like the rigid tress are displaced by the thunderstorms in our lives. The degree of a person's strength is not his brawny power or stiffness, but in his suppleness and compliance with what is beyond control. The trees that danced with the wind were soon erect again. The trees that struggled were destroyed.

When you conform to the natural order of things, you neither go with the flow, nor against it. In submitting to the laws of the universe, you display a sublime trust in the almighty. You create your own flow.

– 15 –

Finding Extraordinary in the Ordinary

Some say "God is in the details," indicating that openings for brilliance and ingenuity come from considering the details. However, the paradox is; in this fast paced world not many have the inclination to look into the details. There is clamour all around urging us to do something great, to live life king size, however, those seeking extraordinary feats, position, triumph, recognition or returns are exposed to soul-numbing burdens and stresses that detaches them from the moment, the now, the present.

My father takes a deep delight in the small and ordinary things. He can work an entire morning cleaning the little piece of land around his home, or in rearranging his book case. He also enjoys observing and connecting with nature and considers this time a time well spent.

He often tells me that one doesn't need to jump higher than anyone to see the sunrise and sunset. He loves being with his thoughts, his books at home, in the sanctuary he's created within its walls. This simple life has provided him with extraordinary insight into the natural and human condition. Nature often acts as a backdrop in his conversations about life and living. He once told me about the Golden Oriole.

In the ordinary canopy of his tree top home, where the rays of the sun dance but don't quite penetrate, rests the perfectly extraordinary golden oriole with his less-colourful mate. The golden oriole is a small class of bird found throughout Europe and western Asia. The male golden oriole Bird is astonishing with prominent yellow and black feathers. Both the male and female however, are hard to spot in the awning as they are not only camouflaged amongst the leaves but also by the golden rays of the run. How extraordinary to be camouflaged in and by the sun, and yet perfectly ordinary.

My father is able to provide such simple yet powerful insights as he believes we become extraordinary simply by opening our eyes and hearts to the wonders integral to every moment. One does not require any special skill to appreciate the tranquillity of the moment, no degree is required to appreciate the wonder of being present, being cognizant of ourselves, nature and the universe. "Think of the small as large" says Lao Tzu and the ordinary becomes extraordinary.

Follow Your Heart: It Knows the Way

It really doesn't matter where a story is born, whether it is a conversant legend or a personal reminiscence, the telling and retelling typifies the connecting of dots and before we know it once upon a time comes to stand for some recurring truth. Stories speak louder than words and this one in particular urges us to not let the noise of others' opinions drown out one's inner voice.

A group of frogs were roaming through the thickets, when two of them fell into a deep quarry. All the other frogs congregated around the pit. At first they thought of helping the frogs out, however, when they saw how deep the pit really was they all gave a sigh of resignation. They conveyed their despondency to the two frogs in the ditch by telling them that there was really no hope for them and they might as well resign themselves to their fate. The two frogs disregarded the despairing comments made by their peers and tried to jump up out of the pit. The other frogs, who saw this as an exercise in futility kept telling them to stop, and that they should stop hurting themselves and give in to their kismet. Finally, one of the frogs took notice of what the other frogs were saying and stopped trying. She fell down spent. The other frog continued to jump as hard as he could. Once again, the throng of frogs shrieked and gesticulated from above asking the frog to stop hurting himself. "Can't you see what will eventually happen? Look at your dead friend. Please stop". The frog in the pit however, began jumping even harder and finally in one last shove made it out of the ditch. When he got out, the other frogs looked perplexed, "Did you not hear us?" they asked. Only when the frog didn't answer they realized that he was deaf.

More often than not voices from outside dilute your standpoint. You need to stand firm in the certainty of your voice and journey through life without attachment to the validation of others. Let your heart guide you.

After all a good heart, a robust heart is better than all the heads in the world.

– 17 –

It is in Giving That We Receive

In a land not too far away a wise man once distributed some excellent quality seeds to the heads of the two communities who resided in the vicinity. He told them that the seeds would produce corn so lovely that the entire locale would look like it was spun of gold. Happily the two leaders planted the seeds and waited.

In the harvest season their fields indeed looked like liquid gold when the crops swayed in the languid breeze. Other members of the locality also got excited about this venture. The heads then distributed the seeds from their own harvest in their communities.

The results were brilliant the first year, however, in subsequent years the crops of one community continued to flourish while the yield from the other community declined in terms of quality. Everyone debated on the plausible reasons for this occurrence. After all, the lands were the same in terms of fecundity and environs. Even as they contemplated and deliberated, the wise man visited them again.

He took one look at the produce and smiled sadly. He said "You have not been sharing your bounty as you should have" Mystified by his summation both the leaders argued "But we both shared our seeds with the people of our community." The wise man replied "One of you has been sharing the best of his corn seeds with the farmers in his neighborhood while the other has been keeping the best for himself and sharing the seeds of inferior quality from the produce with them". He looked at his baffled audience and continued "The results are visible, the wind picks up the pollen and carries it from field to field. So if your neighbors grow inferior corn, the cross-pollination brings down the quality of your own corn. This explains why the corn in one community has thrived while the other has weakened".

Nature has made you a giver, your hands are born open, and so is your heart. There may be times when your hands are empty, but despite that when you give without considering your own loss or gain, give without seeking, give the best that you can- your heart and eventually your hands will always be full.

A Chance at Living Many Lives

The idea to write this article came from a seemingly mundane query. A parent of my student questioned me on the relevance of a particular text prescribed in the syllabus. This was not a new question to me, having taught literature to high school students for more than 15 years now. Often parents interrogate the bearing of classics like 'Jane Eyre', 'Wuthering Heights' and 'Shakespeare' in today's world and /or worry about the explicit sensual content in novels like 'The Kiss of the Spider Woman' and 'Like Water for Chocolate' impacting their child's impressionable minds. These interrogations become particularly pertinent when they see their child struggling to acquire a higher grade in English, a subject they don't often consider vital when equated with the sciences and mathematics.

Over the years my answer to each parent has more or less remained the same. Where else I say but in books can you truly escape to another land, another dwelling, and another time and come back relatively unscathed? Where else but in books can you find both provocation and privacy? Where else can you examine something fragile and tentative without the fear of breaking it? Reading and analysing books is the only way students can move away from the prescribed journey and yet remain on track.

Today we are dealing with a paradox of sorts. The world is now becoming a global village, yet the youth is becoming more introvert and unilateral. It is mostly through the different novels they study, that students get to live the life and experience the priorities and dilemmas of a diverse individual. This forces them out of their comfort zones, albeit in imagination, and embarks them on an empirical journey. What makes this journey particularly meaningful is the discussion of the text in class. The dialogue not only sheds inhibitions and underscores universal themes but also provides a mountain of perspectives that prepares them for their individual paths ahead. Scott Fitzgerald says "That is part of the beauty of all literature. You discover that your longings are universal longings, that you're not lonely and isolated from anyone. You belong."

To provide an analogy; when we travel rich, we meet other rich people who live in similar opulent hotels and share parallel experiences. This familiarity might be contented and fun but in no way does it broaden our worldview or make us rich in experience. When we travel poor we meet people from all walks of life, each in his own private heaven or hell, each with a story very dissimilar to ours. Our mode of transportation (although bumpy) could offer us vistas that we might have never imagined. The soaking in of the local flavour and culture only happens when we do not just put the tip of our foot in the water but jump right in. We soak in humanity. Students today are travelling rich and exposure to different novels allows them an opportunity to travel poor.

I also reiterate that there is no wrong book. 'Wuthering Heights' in its morbid and gothic elements hides the transcendental nature of love and 'Jane Eyre' carries in its many pages lessons on beauty in simplicity. Shakespeare shows us how absolute power corrupts absolutely and the sensuality in 'The Kiss of the Spider Woman' accentuates the need of all humans to find an escape. This is just naming the usual suspects. There are so many lovely novels that could and should be deliberated upon. Each book makes you live a new life, a new experience and what's more? The book never really ends. It grows inside you and around you and without you even realizing it helps you grow.

Most parents are convinced with this answer and to those who still have reservations, I say welcome to my class. Take a ride with these books and decide for yourself.

This pretty much clinches the deal.

– 19 –

From a Child's Mouth

Muhammad Ali once said, "Children make you want to start life over". This simple yet profound statement resonates within the walls of my home almost every day as I interact with my daughters. Often, I try to give them precepts on life, however, it is they who inadvertently teach me what life and living is all about. The unvarnished truth, lessons on humility, tenacity of purpose and objectivity are only some of the life lessons that my children have imparted to me. Listening to them gives me a fresh perspective, and washes away any angst that might have accumulated over time.

For the Annual Day in school, my younger daughter had been given a part in the play based on the novel 'Matilda' by Roald Dhal. She was extremely excited as it also happened to be one of her favourite books. To ensure that one student did not have too many lines to learn; each character was played by two or more students depending on the length of the role. One of her classmates and my daughter were given the role of Ms. Trunchbull, the mean headmistress in the novel. My daughter got two scenes and her classmate got two. Things progressed well. However, just a week before the enactment of the play, my daughter came back home looking hurt and sad. When questioned she told me that one of her scenes had been given to the other Ms. Trunchbull, so now her classmate had three scenes and my daughter had one.

As is the prerogative of a mother, my hurt and sadness was more acute than that of my daughter. Not only did it seem unfair but this change in the eleventh hour I rationalized would put a dent in my daughter's morale. I decided to contact the teacher and ask her for a rationale behind her decision. My daughter however, discouraged me. "Please don't ask my teacher anything" she said. "Why"? I questioned. "Aren't you upset about this? Don't you want to resolve this?" "I am upset Mama, however, there is nothing to resolve". Her response baffled me and we got into a conversation that resulted in astounding results.

"It is simple she said. The other girl was doing a better job than me. She is a better actor than me. Yes, I do feel a little sad but what ultimately matters is, that our play does well. If I get my part back but the play does not go well I will be even more disappointed".

All I could do was hug her tightly as in the face of her wisdom my words seemed juvenile. Her big picture thinking completely demolished my detail oriented perception. Often in our personal agendas and pursuits we forget what we really need to focus on. It is the simple mind of a child that has the potential to look beyond the unproductive and concentrate on the truly relevant things in life. As adults we become more and more self-seeking in our thought process and a child can take us back to the basics to reveal the joys of shared responsibility and collective success.

– 20 –

Happily Married?

During a conversation with a young friend we stumbled upon the topic of marriage. He at the moment is single and not in any kind of rush to get hitched. I, on the other hand, have been married for good many years. It was no surprise that we agreed to disagree on more than a couple of things. My friend saw marriage as an exam that he felt had a 50 percent chance of failure if attempted without the essential groundwork. He worried about things not being perfect, of two people cogently trying to dance a duet when all they were good at was dancing solo. He was apprehensive of rushing into a binding commitment without considering all the pros and cons. When I tried to tell him, that marriage is probably one's best chance to grow up he scoffed and said, "Of course you would say that…you're happily married"

I later deliberated how it's always, 'happily married' in terms of married couples, however, no such adjective is attributed to any other relationship. Ever heard of 'Happily friends'? No relationship is always happy, or forever balanced (fifty-fifty) - especially a marriage. It's always seventy-thirty, or sixty-forty or occasionally even eighty-twenty. Someone pulls the weight sometimes while the other is a drag. Someone puts someone else up on a dais while remaining behind the stage. Someone works very hard to keep the boat sailing while the other just dances with the waves. And suddenly, the roles are reversed. Trials and tribulations are palpable in all relationships and marriage is no exception. Instead of having idealistic notions about marriage one should see it like any other relationship that consolidates, rejuvenates, disintegrates, stagnates and educates depending on what one brings to it. It is not chains or best laid plans or even mutual interests that hold a marriage together. It is threads - hundreds of tiny threads, one's disposition and friendship that sew people together over the years.

One of my go to books 'The Prophet' by Kahlil Gibran best elucidates the concepts of marriage; which holds true for any lasting relationship. "*Let there be spaces in your togetherness, Fill each other's cup but drink not from one cup. And stand together, yet not too near together: For the pillars of the temple stand apart, and the oak tree and the cypress grow not in each other's shadow."* When we BUILD a home, we start with desire and determination to make it happen. Initially one's dream home could look like rubble and sweat and dust. Even the best blueprints might be thwarted. But once the dust clears and the desire and determination consolidate; the rubble will take shape. Similarly, a marriage especially in the beginning might look amorphous. What finally gives it shape is not something external, but that which we carry in our hearts and minds. We are not always beings of logic, but rather beings of emotion and home is not a place but a feeling.

I'm not compelling my friend to tread unfamiliar waters, I'm trying at being a lighthouse in case his ship sets sail.

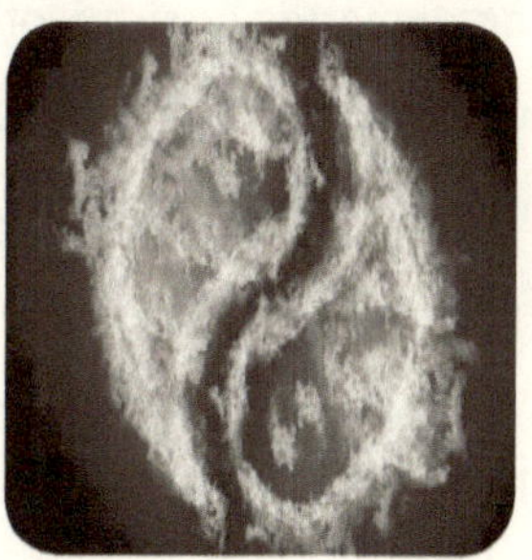

– 21 –

Home is Where You Find It

Life is what happens to you when you are too busy making other plans. It surprises you with unexpected gifts, with curve balls that underscore the extraordinary in the ordinary. Alternately, the pace of life today is hectic and in meeting the demands of time, often the essentials are overlooked or not emphasised enough. Add to this the self-seeking mindset and life style that erodes the very keystones that a family rests upon. In my home, everyone has their own room or a place that is their favourite haunt. We are all separated by the very walls that hold the foundation of our home together. Sometimes, it's only at dinner that we meet, have hurried and often silent meals together, preoccupied with things that need to be done. The sad part is that we don't even realise that we are silently drifting apart.

Travelling undoubtedly gives us a chance to discover and explore more around us, however, it can also become a medium to unearth what's inside us. This is the beauty of life; it teaches us in multifarious ways. Our summer holiday provided a fresh perspective in a way we least expected. We had decided to go to Singapore and Malaysia to enjoy the pristine beaches and theme parks. Since Singapore is somewhat compact, the room of the hotel we booked online was rather small. It necessitated that we all share the same living space and the diminutive bathroom. It also dictated that we interact with each other all the time as we were literally at an arm's distance from each other. We were forced to come to a consensus regarding what programs to watch on TV, what to eat, share our reactions at what we saw and felt. It initially felt like an irksome exercise but eventually turned out to be the proverbial blessing in disguise. Yes, there were altercations but there were also meaningful conversations and all because the physical walls that separated us in our own home were no longer there.

As we sat for meals together, we laughed at each other's antics and idiosyncrasies that we had long forgotten. As we packed and unpacked suitcases we did the same with little snippets and stories. We felt the compatible silence as we relaxed together after a particularly tiring day. We suddenly had time to give informed responses, listen to each other and take pictures galore. It was almost like we were getting to know each other again.

I knew that once we got back home, this magical mystical time would evaporate and the fabric of our life would again be coloured by the hectic pace that we move in. However, I also knew that in that capsule of time we had not only found entertainment and escape but also regained a sense of family. Time that erodes memories, can also help us make new ones. All we must do is travel to known and unknown destinations together again. After all, it's not the destination, not even the journey but the people that we travel with that give meaning and rekindling to life.

- 22 -

Insight

The Japanese believe suffering some kind of impairment and having a history, a story to tell, augments the exquisiteness of an object. This is the reason why when they restore broken objects they glorify the impairment by filling the cracks with gold. The object then becomes more valuable as it carries in its realm a story, a lesson, a dignity that would have paled in its initial brilliance

I wonder what we see when we perceive broken objects or effects rendered worthless with time. Do we see wasted beauty, faded glory, an imperfection in our otherwise seemingly perfect world? Or do we see a capsule in time, a joyful memory, a poignant moment?

Beauty lies in the eye of the beholder they say, however, if the eye is the window to the soul then our soul/psyche is in some way connected to the beauty we perceive around us. If our inner being is elevated, is beautiful, we will find ourselves in a plane where nothing is ugly or meaningless. Each fallen leaf will talk of sagacity and experience. A wrinkled face will be a map to known and unknown destinations. A torn page will be a part of a story that has fed the imagination of generations. A puddle of water will be a celebration of rain and a rough terrain will be an opportunity to experience new vistas. Our perception changes it all.

Still waters run deep. Appearances can be misleading and our attachment to them will make us live shallow lives. To find depth and meaning we need to look beyond exteriors. When we find extraordinary in the things that seem conventional we live unusual lives. The splendour we determine around us percolates into our own lives and we find beauty inside us, in our very existence. This then starts a benevolent circle that energises the heart and minds and helps us create exquisiteness in and around us. An anonymous writer says "The way to love someone is to lightly run your fingers over that person's soul until you find a crack, and then gently pour your love into that crack."

Next time you see impairment, don't turn away from it. Instead see the beauty, the story, the wisdom and the wonder it hides in its crevices.

– 23 –

Don't Miss the Signs

Every once in a while, we all encounter occurrences that seem more than just coincidences, however, in our race to reach the destination we often overlook the signs that might have helped us navigate our journey better. Sometimes we just don't want to see what stands right in front of us, or we simply want what we want, when we want it. Then if a sign coincides with our desire, we peg it as real. If it doesn't, we ignore it, often facing grave ramifications.

What do you do when your car breaks down? In most cases the driver gets out of the car shaking his head at this aggravation and looks under the bonnet of the car as though the mysteries of the engine and the car will reveal themselves. At some point however, the driver realises that the obscurities are not about to expose themselves. Besides his looking under the hood, was an exercise in habit and not expertise. He then dials for the mechanic who grudgingly appears and again looks under the hood. He shakes his head, not out of annoyance but out of resignation. He sagaciously says "Before the car completely breaks down…it makes noises …the noises are sporadic initially, however, soon they become intense. If you are in tune with your car, you can predict beforehand that trouble is brewing and that your car needs servicing. It is only when you are so self- absorbed that you miss the signs that result in the car breaking down in the middle of no-where". Resolving to be more in tune with the 'sounds' of your car you get back behind the wheel and speed up to put this incident behind you.

The mechanic's words ring true and there is a lesson for all of us in this not so hypothetical situation. It takes an open heart, a supple and obedient heart to notice the signs God sends, and then to swell with courage or gratitude in response. We human beings possess divine wisdom, an ability to be mindful and read the signs imbued in the progressive depths of our souls. All we need to do is stay attuned to the 'sounds' that our engine makes despite the noise generated by the chaos of our life.

– 24 –

Journey Into Yourself

There is a difference between being found and finding yourself. Imagine how rewarding and beautiful a journey could be; a journey in which instead of travelling outward, you travel inward and find that everything you were in pursuit of was already within you.

An old fable goes like this. Ten learned men were braving a rough terrain in their quest for enlightenment. At one point they needed to cross a surging, turbulent river. They made a human chain of sorts and somehow managed to cross the river. Since the gushing waters had made communication impossible they decided to ensure that each one of them had made it safely across the river. They took turns in counting and to everyone's dismay found that they could count only till nine. The tenth person was missing. They despondently hung their heads and wondered if they should continue their journey. A young boy, who was passing along, stopped and saw the misery on their faces. "What happened? Why do you all look so sad?" he asked. "We've lost our friend to the river" they said. "There were ten of us when we started and now we are only nine". The boy looked at them quizzically. "I think I can find your friend" he stated. The wise men looked astounded. "How"? they questioned. The boy asked all of them to stand in a line. Then he began counting and voila! he counted till ten. The men were stunned and fell at his feet. "You got our friend back to us. You are a miracle worker" they said in unison. They boy only smiled and continued his journey.

It was only after he left that realization dawned; while counting the others each of them had forgotten to count themselves

So often in meeting the demands of life and time we forget to count ourselves. Our obsession with what's outside creates complexity that robs us of our innate simplicity and wisdom. Like the 'learned' men we panic about something that isn't lost. As we begin simplifying things, begin looking inwards, we move closer to the basics. As we move closer to the basics we see things as they really are. As we see things with more clarity, we find ourselves. Everything else follows.

– 25 –

Kindness of a Stranger

This incident happened a long time ago, during a chilly winter in Buffalo, New York. Yet, it often envelops my mind especially during the turn of the year when we look out upon the world's hectic life and become more interested in people than in things. As I consider making new resolutions, remembering to be kind stays on top of the list.

My husband and I, a young couple then were the proud owners of our first home in the suburbs of Buffalo. The house was a beautiful raised ranch, however it had some obvious defects which we overlooked due to our excitement and inexperience. About 2 weeks after buying the house we realized that it needed a new furnace. Since a new furnace seemed rather expensive, we decided to get it repaired.

On a cold December afternoon when the mechanic came home my husband was away at work. Since the furnace was in the garage, I stepped out to direct him. As he examined the furnace, I stood shivering in the wind. "Young lady" he said, "this may take a while, you might want to step in and get a jacket". As I turned towards the door I realized I had locked myself out. The mechanics of the door and the latch were still new to me. While I was trying to think of a way out of my predicament, the mechanic came out of the garage. I didn't say a single word and yet he figured out exactly what had transpired. He asked me where my husband worked and how long it would take him to get home. When he found out that it would take him about 45 minutes to come home he looked perplexed. "I have to go to another job site, otherwise I would have asked you to sit in my truck… its heated" he said clearly uncomfortable. "I'll be fine" I said. I was not really his problem, yet he seemed hesitant to leave. He went towards his truck, then walked back to me…removed the colossal jacket he was wearing and all but shoved it into my hands. "Wear this till your husband comes home".

"I'll be fine" I insisted and shook my head. He thrust the jacket in my hands. "I'll pick it up if and when I come this side" were his parting words. I'm not sure he heard my half frozen "Thank you". My husband found me 30 minutes later warm and snug like a bug in a rug. The jacket covered me entirely.

Later, when we didn't hear from him we tried contacting him through the agency, however, it was futile. I held on to the jacket for a while and then a few years later I gave it to someone in need. Around the same time every year, I am reminded of this incident and a feeling of warmth envelopes me. I am reminded to be a little kinder than I need to be. I am also reminded of the fact that even though the human body has limitations, the human spirit is made boundless through kindness.

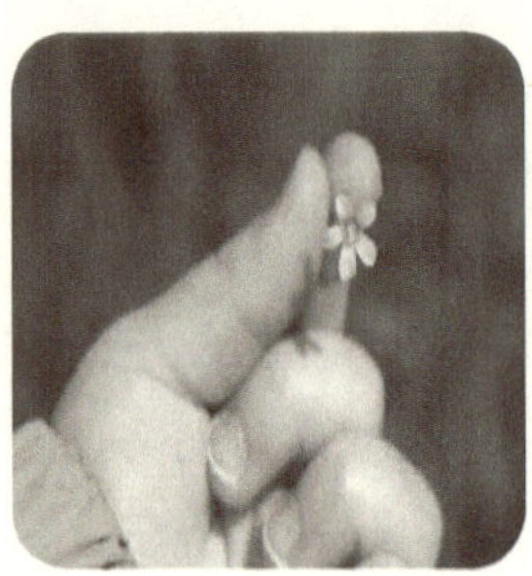

- 26 -

Labour of Love

The mighty Himalayas, the abode of the Gods beckon those seeking meaning and salvation in life. A parable from this divine region goes like this; A man disenchanted by wealth and power began his journey towards the Himalayas. As he trudged along the steep slopes, he notices a girl (about 10 years old) carrying her younger brother on her back climbing alongside him. Her brother was a ruddy faced child and healthy as only the people of the hills can be. The girl was bent by the effort, full of sweat and grime and yet she smiled as she scaled the difficult path. The man patronizingly ruffled the little boy's hair and said; "He must be a huge burden to carry on this rough terrain". The girl stopped abruptly. She looked crestfallen. "Burden? How? He is my brother sir and I love him. Where there is love, there is no burden. I could carry him for miles and not get tired".

The man was stunned into silence. He understood that only love has the power to make such forbearance possible. Realization dawned that the moments in his life when he felt the weight of the world upon his shoulders were only moments that manifested the absence of love.

When one is stirred by a great resolve, moved by love and passion, the obstacles in the path become cornerstones of a meaningful journey. Your mind transcends limitations, your consciousness expands in every direction and you find yourself in a new, great and wonderful world. Once it is touched by love, the work that you do is no longer a means to an end but fruition, relaxation and salvation all rolled into one. It is no longer something that you do but rather something that you are; something that you have potential to become.

You can either view yourself as someone who sweeps the dirty roads or as someone who presents the world with benign fresh start every morning. You can see yourself as a banal teacher or a pathbreaker who reveals numerous and wonderous trails to young, enthusiastic minds. When you find meaning in what you do the entire universe resolves the paradox for you; when there is love there is no labor!

Lemon Tree

For a long long time no lemons grew in the tree we planted in our front yard. We waited with anticipation, however, we were seasonally disappointed. When we had almost given up, unexpectedly, the tree surprised us with lemons. Not just a few, but with an overabundance of the lemon fruit.

The natural fecundity of the tree fascinated everyone. Since the fruit dangled into the pavement adjoining our yard, it was accessible to anyone who passed by. People did pass by and often helped themselves to the lemons hanging on the tree. Initially, we didn't mind, however, when the pilfering of fruit became rampant I felt the need to protect our lemons.

Now, at first I tried putting a sign, later I told the security guard to watch out and when that didn't work I grumbled every time I could. At some point my husband grew tired of my constant complaining.

"Don't you remember the time the tree bore no fruit, now that it is flourishing, what is the harm if the fruits are shared with others?"

"I don't mind sharing the lemons" I said "what bothers me that people are just taking without consent".

My perceptive husband replied; "You had no control over the tree when it bore no fruit and likewise you have no control over who eats the fruit now. The lemons will go to whoever needs them. It is the will of God, that got us lemons in the first place and the spirit of God prevails even now. It is a privilege that we were a part of his divine plan".

I felt like Simba in a particularly moving yet insightful scene from the movie 'Lion King'. Mufasa tells little Simba "A king does not think about what he can take from his land, or what his people can offer him, but rather what he can give to his land and people". Just like Simba nods is acquiescence, I too succumbed to this divine deliberation.

I realized that the lemon tree was just a manifestation of how God uses us as instruments to serve his purpose. I also understood that when we receive gratefully and give happily we create an environment where benevolence can flourish. In this environment, lemon trees suddenly come to blossom and everyone is blessed.

ism - 28 -

Let It Go

The popular refrain from the Disney movie 'Frozen' tricochets..."let it go...let it go". We croon along without really internalizing or even paying attention to the notion it propagates. Letting go is perhaps not as easy as the song makes it sound. Here is a parable that helps us introspect.

While on a journey two monks came across an overflowing river. It was certainly an uphill if not impossible task to cross the river. But the monks were strong. Their arduous, austere and principled life had made them physically and mentally resilient. What however, made their task rather trying was the fact that they were faced by a moral dilemma. There were two women who needed to cross the river too. It would be dishonourable to leave them behind yet since they were monks: propriety demanded that they do not touch the women.

Both were contemplative for a while. Soon however, Monk 1 went to the hapless women- carried one in his arms and put her down across the river. He came back and helped the other woman in the same manner while monk 2 watched him with utter disdain. The profuse thanking by the women did nothing to mitigate his scorn.

The monks continued on their journey. As the day drew to a close, the brilliant sunset was lost on monk 2 who had been unduly reticent and perturbed. Finally, he asked his companion- "You know we are not to touch women...why did you carry them?" Monk 1 smiled. It was a smile that resonated with sagacity and acquiescence. He said "I left those women by the river...you my friend, are still carrying them"

Often and sometimes unknowingly, like monk 2 we carry an invisible baggage that weighs us down in our journey of life. Anger, resentment, regret, grief and hurt often envelope us as we trudge along. They are just as attached to us as our own limbs and it is hard for us to set them aside. We nurture a futile angst for what could have been or for the road less travelled. Caught between limited free will and the play of destiny we ponder for too long, try to fix what is not broken and emerge cynical and sceptical. We need to let go. It is not an option. It is a mandate for one who wants to live without shackles.

It is not the journey that wears us out…it is a grain of sand in our shoe. We need to dust out this sand, clear the cobwebs, and shake off the remnants of our past misgivings. The English rock band Oasis got it just right in their song- "just take what you need and be on your way …and stop crying your heart out"

Let Love In

Adulthood undoubtedly comes with many pluses; however, it is also plagued by a few minuses. We finally begin to see the world as it is, and with that revelation comes both joy and despondency. Sometimes we get so jaded and caught up in the prosaic that we forget what it was to see the world with the eyes and heart of a child and imagine what the world could be without being unduly concerned by what it is.

A diminutive story I read by a Japanese author points to the fact that so absorbed are we by the realities of life that we fail to see magic even when it visits us at close quarters.

The simple story goes like this; a young boy and a girl living in different parts of the globe were connected by one tenuous thread. Each believed that they had a soul mate, one person in this world who was 100% meant for them. Although they knew not at the moment who this person was or of each other, yet their belief carried them through life. It could only be divine intervention that they accidentally met each other and felt the intense tug of compatibility. When they disclosed to each other what they had grown up believing, they could hardly believe their luck; they had actually met each other- the one person meant for them. They had a rapturous conversation for about 10 minutes. After which however, doubt set in. Both began to wonder how it could be so easy for them to meet each other. The path of true love is known to be strewn with thorns. If love had come to them so effortlessly, was it true love? When the doubt could not be abated, they decided to put themselves through a test. They decided to go their separate ways without disclosing any details about themselves to each other. If they were meant to be together, they would surely find each other again. What they didn't realize then was that the cosmos had already conspired to unite them-they had already found each other. It was unlikely that this chance would come to them again. The story ended on a sad note; they departed never to meet again.

So accustomed are we to the grim realities, practicality and routine of our lives that we have misgiving about miracles when they attempt to illuminate our lives. If we can hold on to our childlike sensibilities, our faith, and gratitude God will open avenues for us that we could never imagine on our own. However, if we are continuously assailed by suspicions, then even open doors might close never to open again. Life changes very quickly, in a negative way, if you let it; Life also changes very quickly, in a positive way, if you let it. Let love in.

- 30 -

Giving Meaning to Your Life

"Let the beauty of what you love be what you do."

– Rumi

Unlocking our own potential is a desire that fuels our hearts as we navigate through life. Each of us seek fulfilment by perusing tasks that give meaning to our life. For some it could be climbing mountains and for others planting a rose garden. It is our myriad interests and personalities that provide contrasts that not only raise interesting issues but are seminal to life itself. Although I enjoy the deliberations and dialogs brought forward by such disparities, working women vs. homemakers is the kind of debate I avoid simply because I have deep respect for both.

I understand, a housewife can look after her family in a more effective way. She is there 24/7 for her kids and family. She gets to decorate and redecorate her house, she takes up new hobbies and learns new skills. She manages the challenges at home and finds meaningful ways to manage her time.

A working woman on the other walks the thin rope between her work place and at home. She pretty much needs to do what a homemaker does and at the same time works at maintaining her professional career. Like a skilled juggler she performs again and again without ever letting the ball drop.

A case in point would be my mother. In the early nineteen seventies when she took up teaching some eye brows were raised and once we (her children) came along there were serious frowns. She was counselled time and time again to give up her work, however, she held her ground. She wanted to provide the best education for her children which necessitated a better income and also wanted to forge an identity for herself. All her sacrifices, her seamless changing of roles, her tenacity of purpose did not go in vain. Through her grit and resilience she excelled both at her work and at home. She led by example and showed us the importance of being independent, of being focussed and of pursuing goals whatever they might be. It was amazing to see how she was always there for us despite having a full time job and other responsibilities in and around the house. She showed us through every word and action that the delicate balance between home and a work place could be achieved. She also inculcated in us a deep respect for home makers as she often eulogized her own mother who was a house wife. My mother retired recently, as the Principal of a government school and needless to say I am very very proud of her.

My own zeal to maintain a work life balance and excel comes from the legacy that my mother has bequeathed us. Similarly, my sister is a passionate home maker and visiting her home is always a delight.

Coming back to the central idea, whether we are homemakers or professionals, we need to be passionate about what we do. We need to seek meaning and purpose in our everyday so that we can leave behind a legacy that is etched into the minds of others and the stories they share about us. It shouldn't be too hard, after all, what we seek is also seeking us.

Let There Be Light

Diwali, the festival of lights is celebrated with much fervor and delight in various regions across India; as symbolic of not only the triumph of good over evil, but also as indicative of the enlightenment of soul. There are numerous mythological parables associated with the revelries and sacraments observed on this day among which these four are the most prominent. Lord Rama returned to Ayodhya after 14 years of exile and after defeating Ravan who abducted his wife Sita. Pandavas are said to have come out of the forest after their 12-year banishment, during which they faced not only extenuating circumstances but also several threats on their lives. Lord Vishnu in his 8th incarnation as Krishna destroyed the demon Narkasura after travelling all the way from Dwaraka in Gujarat to Kamaroop in Assam.

Goddess Lakshmi emerged from the Milky Ocean when Devas and Asuras churned the ocean for Amrutha-ambrosia.

All the above legends celebrate the conquest of not only the darkness that exists externally but also underscore the resolve to overcome the darkness within. They give us a reason to celebrate and a cause to contemplate and reflect upon the grit and tenacity that makes such victories possible. It took Lord Ram 14 years of living in the forest, heartache of losing his wife and fighting the demonic Ravan to arrive at his day of triumph. Similarly, Pandavas lived in disguise, in danger, in debilitating conditions and sometimes in abject shame to finally reclaim their throne. It is only after great dissonance; agitating the mighty ocean that nectar was found.

Great things take time, perseverance and diligence. Diwali then is not only about celebrating victory but also about rejoicing in the resilience of the human spirit that can find meaning and purpose in enervating circumstances. This festival is also about the fruits of patience that come to those who trust in the divine order. It teaches us that no matter how extended and murky the night; it will always be overcome by the day. Sometimes life may make us feel that we are exiled to a forest with no respite like Rama, or that we have lost something that was right fully ours like the Pandavas. Like Lord Krishna we might have to face arduous journeys to reach our destination; or feel the acerbic pull and push of life in search of nectar. In these trying times we must remember the message that these stories communicate - no matter how dark the night, if there is light in your heart, you will find your way home.

- 32 -

Life Begins at the End of
Your Comfort Zone

I studied in a convent tucked in the verdant foothills of the Himalayas. Nainital was often cocooned in a fog that cloaks the hills and valleys; obscuring the vision. When it rises there is a crispness and clarity in the air. Metaphorically, I'm not sure for how long our childhood remained cloaked in this mist. This literal and metaphoric haze I think first starting lifting in a Hindi class when we realized we were at a threshold where the life as we knew it then was dissipating and the future tickled our young minds.

Our new Hindi teacher Mrs. Maya Ram, was tall, sturdy and formidable not just in appearance but also in disposition. She made us sing the 'Gayatri mantra' at the beginning of the class and ensured that we learnt what it meant by heart. Used to the casual approach of our old Hindi teacher we thought this as intrusion. While we were still deciding whether we feared her, respected her or just plain hated her she came to class with a poem; 'Ek Boond' (A drop) by Ayodhya Singh Upadhyaya "Hariaudh".

Now, Poetry they say can be dangerous, especially beautiful poetry, because it gives the illusion of having had the experience without actually going through it. The sentiment and passion with which she taught us the poem made a dent in our impressionable minds and we realized it was not a lesson in Hindi but a lesson in life.

The poem talked about the feelings of a drop of rain when it is leaving the bosom of the clouds. She contemplates and shivers in fear wondering why she must leave the safety of her home. She is petrified that she might just get lost in the sands of time. Apprehensive about her future, she tries to allay her fears by thinking that she might just land on a lotus blossom. The drop's hesitations at leaving her comfort zone are so vividly elucidated that they resonated with us as at that moment, we felt we were poised to take the world in our young hands.

The drop's fate was important to us as we corroborated it with ours. Mrs. Maya Ram continued to explain; "at that moment came a gust of breeze and carried the drop unheeding to the sea where a beautiful oyster opened. The little drop fell into the oyster where she became a lovely pearl. People often hesitate and worry when they have to leave their homes, but quite often, leaving their comfort zones transforms them like the tiny drop. You can contemplate going back toward safety or move forward toward growth. Growth must be chosen again and again; fear must be overcome again and again. All of you have the potential to become beautiful pearls" she concluded. The class took on a different dimension and meaning. We knew that Mrs. Maya Ram was teaching us more than the poem and we all fell in love with her despite her rather austere ways. The fog lifted. We learnt that there is only one way of finding out what life brings us…by going forward.

Life is a Lesson in Humility

As a eulogy to humility and perseverance the mystic poet Rumi says "Raise your words, not voice. It is rain that grows flowers, not thunder." Often the humble go unnoticed, however, their effort and good deeds speak for themselves.

There were once two pots made of clay. Each hung on the two ends of a pole which the bearer carried across his neck to deliver water to his master. Although they looked identical, one of them had a crack in it, while the other one was flawless. Despite the long walk from the stream to the master's house, the perfect pot always managed to carry a full load of water while the cracked pot delivered only half of what was expected of him. Never the less, the bearer always treated them with equivalence. This went on for a while. The perfect pot believed he was superior and often retorted "What good are you anyway? It takes you two trips to do what I can do in one. You are just a drain to the resources". The cracked pot however, ignored these remarks and continued to tread the path with equanimity. This further annoyed the pot. One day after pooling his courage he decided to speak to the bearer. "I have noticed that the other pot delivers half my load, yet you do not discard it. How can you treat us both in the same manner?" The bearer gently explained "Have you noticed the beautiful flowers along the path to the master's house? Have you also noticed that the flowers only grow on only one side of the path? That is the side of the broken pot. I planted flower seeds on his side of the path, and every day while we walk back from the stream, he's watered them. Everyone admires the flowers and the other pot knows he is responsible for them and yet he is silent"

The beauty of being humble is that nothing will touch you, neither praise nor disgrace; you realize that just like you others are also walking on the path destined for them. Your humility and trust in God will make your frailest moments worthwhile. Flowers will grow where you tread and your journey will become sublime.

- 34 -

Life is But a Game

As a child, what made me particularly happy was when as a special treat my father would decide to take me to his office. It was a treat for two reasons; firstly, because his office was situated in one of the more scenic locales in Nainital. Chestnut tress fringed the beautiful wooden colonial edifice that served as his workplace. The other reason why going to my father's office held such charm for me was the fact that the common areas and lounges at his work place were scattered with chess boards. The game of chess was a matter of habit and anyone who was taking a break could be found seated next to one of these chess boards. Each one seemed engrossed. I didn't quite know how to play the game yet, however, the small black and white squares and the little objects on top held a strange fascination.

If and when my father's colleagues noticed me, they would call me near the table and either explain how each of the 6 dissimilar pieces moved differently or share a strategy that they had made their own. They would tell me that the queen is the most powerful piece. She could move in any one straight direction - forward, backward, sideways, or diagonally - as far as possible as long as she does not move through any of her own pieces. The rook the bishop each had their own special manoeuvres and they would take some pride in sharing some of those manoeuvres with me. All this fascinated me tremendously and each visit to my father's office made me better informed about the game. Since I would watch them play, some of them would indulgently let me play with them for a bit. Although, I was very young, and not much registered I still tried to imitate them. Mostly I lost even before I got a foothold, however, the fascination continued.

I have forgotten now, all that I learnt about chess, however, I still remember some of the lessons I learnt as I tried to understand the game. No one has, for example ever won a game of chess by moving forward alone. Sometimes you have to move backward or side ways to better get a grip of the game. I learnt that is alright to pause in your journey, move back a step reassess your situation and then move ahead. I also learn that each one plays the game differently depending on his or her position and we cannot really predict which way the game will go. At best we can appreciate that each one has his/her special moves which must be respected even as we work on developing our own special moves. Most of all, I leant that you might learn more from a game you lose than from a game you win. Failure, unlike success is a remarkable teacher. The game of chess, I came to understand is a miniature of life itself. Your disposition, adaptability, forethought, manoeuvring failure, keeping what is important safe and respecting the different styles and abilities will determine the kind of player you are. After all, it's not winning or losing but how you play the game that matters.

Life Lessons from Daughters

Imagine this: a mother holding the tiny trusting fingers of her child and taking cautious baby steps into the vast unknown territory called life. It feels just right. Now visualize two little girls holding a mother's hand and helping her navigate the labyrinth of emotions. How does this feel?

It seems it's a parent's prerogative to help children through the ups and downs of life. I'm here to share, how, children knowingly and unknowingly help their parents make sense of their environs by bringing a fresh perspective and clarity to the situation.

My younger daughter Aishi came home one day upset after her play time. One friend in particular had been explicitly "mean" to her and they had a verbal spat. She was crying and was visibly upset. Only a mother's heart understands the helplessness and anguish that comes with not being the centre of the child's universe and of not being able to amend the milieu to suit the child. Despite never having met this friend I disliked her immediately and asked my child to stay away from her. Aishi, however, came to me a few days later with a goofy smile. She was excited she had patched up with this 'mean' friend and that they were happy again together. My antenna was still up and for all purposes I was the quintessential tigress looking out for my cub. "How can you be friends with her again? Don't you remember how you were crying?" I asked. My child guilelessly answered "But mama she said she was sorry". I was so ashamed of myself. All my years of growing up had robbed me of my innocence and childlike ability to forgive and let go. Only a pure heart of a child can teach you the importance of not holding on to grudges and of living in the moment.

Akshi, my older daughter is 13. Yes, the teenage demons haunt my home, however, I'm here to shatter the preconceived notions generally associated with precarious teenage behaviour. She was having a tough time in school and her so called friends had ganged up against her. She was irritable and unusually quiet at home. My heart broke as I saw her grades slipping in school. I wanted to build a protective wall around her…I even suggested a change of school. In a moment of absolute clarity she said "Mama I've made some mistakes too. It's not all their fault. Such things take time to fix". She also said that she had to face the consequences of her mistakes and the few girls who still spoke to her would have to be her solace. I was astounded by her sense of responsibility, mature perspective and by her grit and determination to beat the odds.

Again, I was forced to introspect. Instead of making the child ready for the road ahead I was making the road ready for my child, not really preparing her for the challenges that lay ahead.

Both my daughters have taught me immensely not only about life but also about living it. I cannot go back to the good old days of my childhood but through them I experience the joys of living the simple, uncomplicated life every single day.

The Russian novelist and philosopher Fyodor Dostoyevsky says it all:

"The soul is healed by being with children."

36

Mind Over Matter

Energy is the currency of the universe. When you 'pay' attention to something you 'buy' that experience. You feed it energy, you think about it, act on your thoughts and your actions then carve the path you must walk on. You become that experience. Organically, it becomes imperative that we are selective in what we focus on. Despite this, we let our mind wander into territories that are arid, choppy and even hostile. We perceive so much of our world through our senses that knowingly or unknowingly we become slaves of them. We are manipulated by our very sanities and our thoughts drift like a dry leaf in the currents created by them. Recently, I read an analogy that could educate us about constructing and regulating our sensory experience.

Say, we had to police five different animals from running into the wilderness. It would be a challenging task as each of them would try his or her method and talent at escaping. In attempting to manage them all, we would not only be unsuccessful in keeping them from running into the wilderness, but also lose control over them and eventually over ourselves. In trying to tame them all we would be pulled in different directions generating only unhappiness and chaos. Instead, we could try tethering each of them into a sturdy pole. This way they would still try to escape but would soon learn of their limits and limitations and would tire out. At some point they would sit docile around the pole. Our only task would be to ensure that the pole is solid and strong. Everything else then falls into place.

Our mind is the allegoric pole around which we must tie our senses. All we need to do is make our mind tough and resilient. It will then rein in our thoughts if and when they get out of control. Once the senses understand that their limits and limitations are decided by a robust mind they will no longer try to defy it. Our senses/thoughts thus tamed, we can spend our energy on the more fecund and receptive environs.

Some thoughts need a tongue, some paper and some a tight leash to walk around the garden of our mind, to refocus, revive and rejuvenate.

- 37 -

Miracles Grow Where You Plant Them

. . . .

There was once a river of crystal clear water and the current swept over the creatures along the bottom. Out of habit, fear and the need for survival each creature in its own manner clung tightly to the kindling and rocks of the river, for clinging was all they knew and resisting the current was a way of life for them.

Although they glimpsed the rays of the sun penetrating the water and knew there was light above, no one really tried to let go and realize another way of life. There was one creature however, who was tired of this life of seamless shackles. "I am tired of clinging. There must be more to life than this. Although I cannot see it yet, I trust that the current knows where it is going. I shall let go, and let it take me where it will. Clinging, I shall never know what I am missing"

The other creatures discourages him and said; "Let go? We have seen the ways of the world. If you let go the current will control you and smash you against the rocks. You don't want to die like that ...do you?"

Scared, but not entirely discouraged he heeded them not. He let go saying; "I don't want to die like that but neither do I want to live like this". Predictably, he was pushed against the rocks and debris by the current. He thought of clinging again but the need to seek better horizons was bigger than his fear. In time the current lifted him free from the bottom into the light above, and he could feel the rays of the sun on his bruised body.

The clinging creatures; to whom he was now an alien, cried, "See a miracle! A creature like us, yet he floats blissfully. He has come to save us". The creature said; "I cannot save you. You have to save yourself from the chains you have bound yourself to. Miracles grow where you plant them. The river delights to lift us free, if only we dare let go. Our true work is this journey, this exploration."

The journey itself becomes the destination when we take an honest, a brave step out of our comfort zone.

Music...the Voice of the Soul

At a low point in my life a friend once told me "find Inspiration and solace in music…it will help you tide difficult times." I brushed him off saying only if things were this simple. At that point; thwarted and disgruntled with life, I discounted that an abstract tenuous notion like music could actually be a salve to the soul.

Today, I've come to appreciate that music is not only a powerful medium of communication and expression but that it also hides in its notes and beats; solace, inspiration and wisdom. Often, I find myself going back to my favorite songs and escaping into their enchanted world. The classics always win. The subtle messages, powerful nostalgia, charm and romance of the days gone by never fail to lighten the heart and mind.

A case in point: 'The Gambler' by Kenny Rogers evokes wistfulness and as I hum along the refined message reaches across. The grudges, hurts other inconsequential things fade away. A resolve to keep the sacred close and to discard the unwanted materializes out of thin air. The unexpected wisdom coming from the 'gambler' underscores that life can teach you in multifarious ways.

'Hotel California', is an allegory about hedonism and greed in Southern California in the 1970s. At the time of its release, the Eagles were riding high in the music world, experiencing substantial success at an alarming level. Though they thoroughly enjoyed what destiny threw their way, there was a sense of disquiet as they grappled the pitfalls of a heady triumph. Through this song they sought to pour their restlessness into their music and to warn others about the dark underside of such reverence. Hence the song sagaciously exposes the duality of human nature and of life itself.

The definitive break up song 'Dreams' is written by Stevie Nicks about Lindsay Buckingham towards the end of their relationship when it was at its most turbulent. The metaphorical last line "when the rain washes you clean- you'll know" ends the song on a positive note despite the obvious heartache. Nicks herself said "I put something at the end that says there's hope." Just Like in life, in this song despair and hope combine seamlessly and the result is truly a dream.

The ballad 'November Rain' talks about what it means to be human, to be vulnerable and to be open to whatever life may bring-be it pleasure or pain. It talks of beauty in transience and it is no surprise that this song drizzles quietly into the heart. Nothing lasts forever, is the message this song brings forth in an innocent yet punishing way. The music is soulful and you're caught in a moment that lasts for eternity.

There are many other songs that give shape and meaning to emotions, thoughts and feelings and one must find their own special song. I am truly grateful to my friend whose advice resonates with the hills and valleys of my life.

- 39 -

Natural Order

Nature provides answers to questions that are elemental to life itself. A reading of literature often becomes a medium for nature to both pose and provide solution to these questions. Study of literature not only educates the head alone but also the heart and the mind. It adds reality and depth to life as it does not merely describe it, but also probes at its heart. Discussions that happen in a literature classroom enriches the necessary proficiencies that daily life requires; and it attempts to provide nourishment to the barren landscapes that our lives might become without the right kind of mediation.

While discussing a poem in class we came to understand how nature (including human nature) is pushed to the margins by the unrelenting force of advancement and industrial development. The longing for natural spaces not corrupted by cement was not lost to the class. We further discussed how human intrusion and lack of understanding of the natural order will ultimately bereft humankind of insight that nature so kindly bestows on us.

One of the students shared a pertinent example to underscore the point that the natural order of things must not be disturbed as humans are not quite ready to understand the subtleties of Mother Nature. He mentioned how as a child he and his friends had spotted a bird's nest under the bushes. Curiosity drove them to bring the nest in the open to examine the nestlings more closely. They enjoyed watching the little babies for a while and later got engrossed in playing and forgot about the nest altogether. When they came back after a while two little birds were missing. Perturbed they looked around, however, they could do nothing about the missing nestlings. When the student reached home he discussed the occurrence with his mother; she all but dragged him to the spot where they had left the nest. The nest was still there, however, one more baby bird was missing. After a couple of frantic questions, his mother quickly kept the nest where it was originally placed-under the bushes. Despite this they could not escape the anguished cry of the parent bird on its return.

As they walked home downcast, the student's mother explained "the parent bird instinctively knows where to build a nest to keep it safe from predators. Your lack of awareness upset the normal direction of things"

This incident made a critical impact on the mind of the child, so much so that after almost a decade he was discussing this incident in a literature class. He had understood that natural order encompasses the natural relations of beings to one another and reckless human infringement will only result in heartache.

Reading, reflecting, contemplating and introspecting are the constituents of a literature class; which often underscore the fact that physical universe is an organized system subject to natural (not human) laws. The answers you seek from nature or from a literature class hinge on the questions you pose and on your readiness to receive the responses.

– 40 –

From Nature's Laboratory

Science represents the human craving to understand nature, however, even Albert Einstein came to an understanding that if we look close and deep into nature we will understand not only science but everything better. My husband, (a scientist but not quite Einstein) has a great affinity towards nature. He loves to nurture the little piece of land around our home; his investment in terms of time, effort and patience has paid off and our little garden is a visual delight.

Our gardener well understands my husband's passion. One day he brought a plant he said would cost us 700 rupees. As my husband went in to get the money I was a little apprehensive. "What miracle plant is this?" I asked. He wasn't dismayed by my sarcastic tone. "It **is** a miracle madam he said, this plant flowers only once in 5 years".

"What is the point of buying such an expensive plant if it only flowers once in 5 years?" I asked incredulously. My Gardener was prepared… "Most flowers bloom during season; what's the novelty in that. I have got something exotic and rare, the beauty of which will be unparalleled".

"What is the guarantee that it will bloom in 5 years? I persisted. He sagaciously answered, "there are no guarantees in life, but once the time and environment is right, the southern western Ghats erupt in an explosion of blue and purple, thanks to the kurinji plant, a tiny flower that blossoms just once every 12 years."

Prone to introspection I wondered, what wisdom from a surprising source! Why are we so happy and satisfied by the norm and the ordinary? Why don't we try something different, something exotic in our life even if it means living with no guarantees and delayed gratification?

Nature's laboratory has the answer. A mercurial creature; nature does not request our permission, does not care for our wishes, disregards our concern for her laws and deductions. She just assumes that we will accept her as she is. No questions asked. However, if we do abide by the natural order of things, are patient and trusting – then we'll know in time the tiny seed will reach fruition.

To trust in the laws of nature, in delayed fulfilment is to place your trust in God.

- 41 -

Of Birds and Butterflies

The American all girl band TLC managed to be socially conscious without being overtly didactic and moralizing in their U.S No.1 song "Don't go chasing waterfalls…please stick to the rivers and lakes that you're used to". Although the song subtly underscores the AIDS crisis…the lyrics also hint at not chasing after visions without substance and rationale.

An avid photographer at one point, my husband would go chasing after the butterflies and birds. He would often ponder upon flowers at length and would try to capture their innate beauty and grace through his camera. He firmly believed that honest photographs of both man and nature provide the world a fresh perspective on how the world should actually be seen; in the intricate transient details that salvage eternity. I remember how he dashed after a butterfly or sat still to observe a bird to capture a perfect shot. I also remember being annoyed and feeling disregarded when we developed our films and found that instead of us, seventy percent of the pictures he had taken would depict the flora and fauna of the place we had visited.

It is needless to say that although we had many many beautiful pictures of the wonderful places we visited around the globe, we never quite got the perfect shot. It is only later that we understood that true beauty cannot be captured …you can only live in that fleeting moment and let the beauty resonate in you.

Eventually, we moved on to buy a home fringed by a small piece of land. Not only a nature lover but also blessed with a green thumb my husband worked on that piece of land like an artist reverently works on his canvass. And just like a vibrant image begins to take shape on the canvass, similarly, 'our little garden' began to take form and dimension. Not only was it a kaleidoscope of colours but also a burgeoning of all kinds of leaves and petals. Since this garden was not pruned or manicured the gay abandon of plants held a strange kind of appeal. First came the tiny sparrow, then the gorgeous kingfisher and eventually the monarch butterflies turned the little piece of land into a visual paradise.

However, this time both my husband and I felt no pressing need to capture these moments. We were content to watch these beauties unfold their drama right before our eyes. We had come to an understanding that we don't need to go chase butterflies, if we mend our garden the butterflies will come to us. Hence, we all must cultivate the garden within, and once the garden blossoms; peace, tranquillity, beauty and wisdom will settle inside us just like the dust settles after a rainstorm.

- 42 -

On Learning

Learning requires a basic humility and mental alignment between the educator and the learner. Once we let go of what we think we know, learning flows into us like a river flows into the ocean. These esoteric concepts are best explained in the climatic moments of the epic Ramayan. When Ram finally defeated Ravan it seems that the story reaches its denouement. However, the learnings do not stop there. A very interesting episode centered on the final moments of Ravan underscores the fact that epics like the Ramanyan and the Mahabharat enclose learnings in every turn. Ravan was not only a well –educated Brahmin but had also captivated everyone including Ram with his knowledge and wisdom. His persistence at his own betterment had won him many boons from the Gods. Despite it all however, Ram had to kill Ravan because of his 'Adharmic' deeds elucidating that wisdom needs to be tempered with humility and morality. Conversely, after defeating him, he praised Ravan for his knowledge and counseled his younger brother Lakshman to seek learnings and blessings of the dying Ravan. He believed no other person could teach better than the erudite Brahmin like Ravan.

If lakshman was reluctant and thought the request strange he did not show it. Dutiful and obedient Lakshman stood with joint hands close to the head of the dying Ravan. However, when several minutes passed and Ravan did not say anything Lakshman looked at Ram perplexed. Ram then tolerantly explained to his brother; "Ravan might have made some injudicious choices, however, at the moment he is your Guru. You actions need to be strengthened with respect. 'Gyaan' is not attained standing at the head of the Guru but at his feet"

Thus humbled Lakshman again went to Ravan, this time standing next to his feet. Ravan understood his intent then and spoke to him of wisdom that often gets pronounced in the final moments of one's life.

There is divine beauty in learning and as we take the world in our hands we must do so humbly. Life and people will continue to teach us if we are disposed and willing to learn. Every person we meet in our journey has the potential to be a 'guru', but it takes a 'Ram' to appreciate that.

Life Teaches You When You Are Mindful

"Be happy in the moment, that's enough. Each moment is all we need, not more."

– Mother Teresa

Once we are truly conscious or aware of something beauty and insight is discovered in the most implausible places. Recently and unwittingly I experienced, how by just living and being in the moment, seemingly mundane tasks take on a new dimension and have the power to uplift both physically and emotionally. In this case, a simple talk by an admission's officer from a university became a lesson on life and living.

An admissions officer from a prestigious University was visiting the school I teach in to talk about the admission process and advise students by providing them first hand perspective. Statistically the speaker said about 30 thousand students applied to the university every year out of which there were about 20 thousand that academically suited the university. However, only 7 thousand are seriously considered by the university out of which only 2 thousand get selected every year. There was a clear cut understanding, how the students were narrowed down from 30,000 to 7000, however, there was no specific criteria as to how they further tapered it down from 7000 to 2000. It could be luck he said and refused to explain further. Despite being an admissions officer he acknowledged that he did not know the secret ingredient that bent the odds in the student's favour. He said that the only thing the students could do was to ensure that they made it to the list of 7000 students who would be seriously considered by the University. After which things were out of their control as the X factor remained a mystery.

Technically it was just statistics, and statistics it would remain if I had not been mindful. His rationale made me introspect how often we fret things that are beyond our control. We spent precious time and energy being anxious about situations that we cannot influence. All we can do really is give it our very best and then back off. Nature, destiny or whatever you might call it will take it from there. We have to gracefully relinquish control as more often than not there is precious little we can do.

He also talked about students submitting essays to the university that do not ring true. Their 'voice' does not chime in those essays because who they are and the person they are presenting to the university is not the same. Each individual is unique and their voice must be heard. One has to be true to oneself as the fake is often discovered and rejected. Again all he was doing was telling students to write their own essays and be sincere and exact when writing facts about themselves. A rather commonplace guidance, however, my being immersed in the moment got me intrigued. All of us wear masks and often hide our true selves in order to fit in, or present a different version of ourselves to the world for myriad reasons. Not only does no one get to know the real you, but also, you never give yourself the freedom to be truly you. We must drop these masks as it is our originality that makes us real.

Lastly, he proudly talked about a press conference held at the university which felicitated its two professors, Robert Shiller and James Rothman for winning the Nobel Prize for Economics and Physiology respectively in the year 2013. When the professors were questioned by the press about their next step/plan after reaching the pinnacle of academic success, both the professors answered that they would continue to do what they were doing; go back to class to teach. The humility and simplicity touched me deeply and again I was pushed to contemplate that our quest for excellence, greatness and success should not disconnect us from our roots and the effects that got us this far in the first place.

I came out of that talk contemplative, yet energized. Mindfulness magically turned the ordinary moment into something extraordinary. There is truism in what a spiritual master says "Life is a dance. Mindfulness is witnessing that dance."

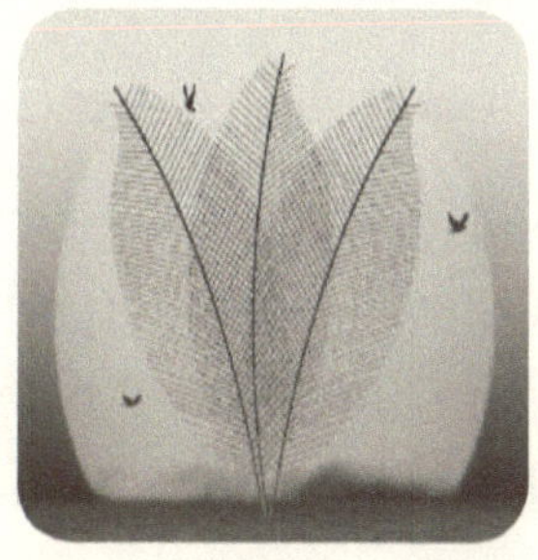

- 44 -

Paper Boats

*S*ometimes *the things we can't change end up changing us.* Childhood is like a favourite season which is transient and yet transcendental. I remember playing in the mud, learning to cycle in rented dented bicycles, getting wet in the rain and listening to the same stories again and again from our grandparents and parents. I particularly, remember racing paper boats in the small drains that would swell with the rains. The fact that nature would eventually take its course and that our boats would sooner or later become pulp did not faze us. So much did we live in the moment that eventuality and consequences meant nothing to us. The sense of wonder, awe and possibility pervaded and insentiently we learnt so much about life and living through these unsupervised jaunts. But seasons change and so do we.

Often, I would find myself nostalgic, wishing for those carefree days for my children too. Maybe, I secretly desired to live my childhood again vicariously through my children. But, the childhood I dreamt about was lost in phones, video games, iPads, and the million T.V channels that entice more than the craggy outdoors. Or so it seemed.

My younger daughter Aishi got an assignment from school, which required her to make boats of different materials and test their durability and adaptability. I all but jumped as this chance to recreate scenarios from my memory, however, imagine my horror when I pleated and creased paper again and again to find that I could not remember how to make a paper boat. I felt mortified as my daughter sat expectantly looking at me. But then help came from unexpected quarters; Technology came to rescue! I quickly found myself opening you tube and searching for a video to make a boat and voila! In no time I had made the paper boat for my daughter. It was truly delightful and as we floated these boats in the buckets filled with water...we laughed and cheered I felt the wonderful memories flood my home.

Life inevitably throws us curve balls; the marvels of daily life are exciting and no one can plan for the unexpected that can transpire in our own home. I've come to understand these curve balls are beautiful reminders that the past, present and future are linked and have no meaning without each other. I understood then that my quandary was that I hated change and loved it at the same time; what I really wanted is for things to remain the same yet get better. This cannot happen. Just like a butterfly cannot shed its wings and go back to the cocoon, similarly, our past must stay where it belongs and the present should take wings. In that moment, I finally grasped that my children will make their own memories which might not be exactly like mine; but will be precious all the same. Their own experiences will inspire the same wonder and awe that I once experienced as a child. And one day life will give them a chance to share this delight with their children in some unexpected moment.

"The only way to make sense out of change is to plunge into it, move with it and join the dance." Alan W. Watts.

– 45 –

Parenting – Means Growing with Your Children

Illustrator and poet Khalil Gibran beautifully describes the relationship between parents and their children. Not only do parents need to bend backwards for their children and then learn to let them go to but must do so with grace, humility and joy. Giving children both roots and wings and lighting their road with possibilities is the proud prerogative of a parent.

> *"You are the bows from which your children*
> *as living arrows are sent forth.*
> *The archer sees the mark upon the path of the infinite,*
> *and He bends you with His might*
> *that His arrows may go swift and far.*
> *Let your bending in the archer's hand be for gladness;"*

My younger daughter was quite animated to go for a 4 day camp organized by her school. Her excitement was slightly discolored by her trepidation as she ventured into the unknown. "Will I have enough clothes? What if the bathroom is messy? What if my friends fight with me? When will you call me?" The questions were relentless. They exasperated me, and yet I couldn't help smiling at her childlike reluctance to step out of her comfort zone - away from home and family.

Although I was almost as worried as she was; I coaxed her, told her of the joys of camping and explained how she would get to spend more time amidst nature and with her friends. I tried to answer her persistent questions with logic and equanimity. I knew it was important that she went for this camp as this was one way she would learn to take her own decisions, albeit small, and manage things on her own. I told her we would talk every day. Despite my best efforts however, as she said 'bye', she said it with some alarm and despondency. Notwithstanding the fact that I knew she would enjoy at the camp the poignancy of the moment did not escape me.

Every evening I spoke to her after dinner and each evening she spoke to me a little less…preoccupied with the occurrences of the day. Once she was back home she was full of 'camp moments'. She kept talking about all the exciting things she did at camp. My role as parent became absolutely certain to me when a few days later I read a message she had written to her friends on my phone. "I miss camp so much" she wrote. Her friends agreed. As an afterthought she wrote later "But I'm also glad to be home". Had she really changed in just 5 days? Was I ready to accept the fact that she had grown to love something independent of her family?

I had to quickly understand that it's not only children who grow. Parents do too. They grow towards understanding when to hold children tight and when to let them take the leap of faith. Parents grow towards being the safety nets that allows their children to take assured steps outside of their comfort zones. Parents also grow towards learning that although they might hold their children's hands for just a little while, they will hold their hearts forever.

- 46 -

Paved Paradise

The horizontal and vertical development of Bangalore fazes me and brings to mind an anecdote that I read recently.

In a city where the thriving population and greed had resulted in concrete jungles, there was a man who envisaged jungles of a different variety. He put all his savings into a ground floor apartment of a building that came with a small piece of land. He believed this gave him a chance to maintain an affinity with the natural world. He put all his heart and soul into that portion of his property determined to make a green patch in an otherwise bleak landscape. His determination and zeal paid off and soon his little garden was a sight that appealed to the eyes of the mind. Momentarily there were butterflies and to his utmost fascination some eggs. He felt he had created a paradise albeit small and tentative. He watched these eggs every day with captivation waiting for new life to emerge out of the world that he had abetted create.

This garden was his baby and he was determined to make everything fall in place. When he saw a little larva struggling to break the egg shell in vain he felt his heart break. Why should this little life have to struggle? Wasn't life difficult enough? He took little tongs and made a tender crack in the egg shell. Surely this would help this little being surface and… voila! It did. Shortly the little larva broke out of the egg and the man was immensely pleased by his role in the larger scheme of things. Happiness is known to be fleeting. The man was disheartened to see that the larva he had helped come into the world had died almost as soon as he came into it. This disillusioned the man who neither understood nor accepted the turn of events.

How was he to know that Mother Nature has a plan? She has given pronounced thought not only to the grander picture but also to the tiniest life force in her design. By pushing its head against the hard shell the larva actually toughens its head which is essential for it to sustain life outside the shell. In his ignorance the man facilitated the death of this larva thinking he was assisting it.

Man's ignorance in the matters of the natural world has left us in a bleak world that we constantly seek escape from. However, the mighty and mysterious power of nature is undefined. Humans foist their perception and construal to the natural world where nothing of human perspective and understanding can apply. Humans are just one of the many species that belong to the natural world. By assuming ourselves to be superior we not only underscore our ignorance but also harm more than we help. This mindless encroachment and meddling with nature will take man to an inevitable stage when nature will eventually either retaliate and prevail (Tsunami, Earthquake etc.) or die a premature and futile death like the larva.

Were we listening when Joni Mitchell said long ago in her song Big Yellow Taxi "We've paved paradise and put up a parking lot"?

Pay It Forward

Mythology claims that sometime before 'The Great War 'between the Kauravas and the Pandavas took place the captivating Karna took a vow of abstinence. He not only gave up meat, wine and women but also offered a beggar or Brahmin whatever they wanted if they came to him while he went to bathe in the Ganga every morning.

Since mystery and speculation always shrouded Karna, predictably, these acts caused a lot of conjecture. Some thought he was just showing off. Other presumed that he did this to please the Gods and increase his powers to defeat/destroy Arjuna. The more astute and perhaps the more sensible guessed that he was simply doing this because he knew that it was unlikely he came out of the battle unscathed or alive. This was probably his way of atoning his past misdeeds, finding peace in his life and hopefully his afterlife.

As we often perceive, people wear kindness like a mantle to redress transgressions or seek favours from the almighty. If virtues are thus rapidly rewarded and kindness affords proximity to God then wouldn't it be simpler if we practiced kindness as a way of life and not just as a bargaining tool?

Why go back thousands of years, sometime in the year 2000, Kevin Spacey and Helen Hunt starrer movie 'Pay it Forward' came in the cinemas. The concept behind it was simple yet innovative. Instead of returning a favour done to you, you needed to do a good deed for three people who in turn would go ahead and do something worthwhile for three other people. Hence these random acts of kindness or benevolent deeds would proliferate and eventually restore our lost faith in mankind. In the larger scheme of things, everything is connected and the good that we do might not have an immediate impact but in due course the ripples will become waves and drench us all in kindness.

In this world that is increasingly unkind, our best defence if to be a little kinder than we must. Like in Karna's story people will speculate and accuse us of selfish ulterior motives. And again, just like Karna, we should disregard doubt, hold the secret to our heart and continue to either pave way for kindness or walk the path ourselves.

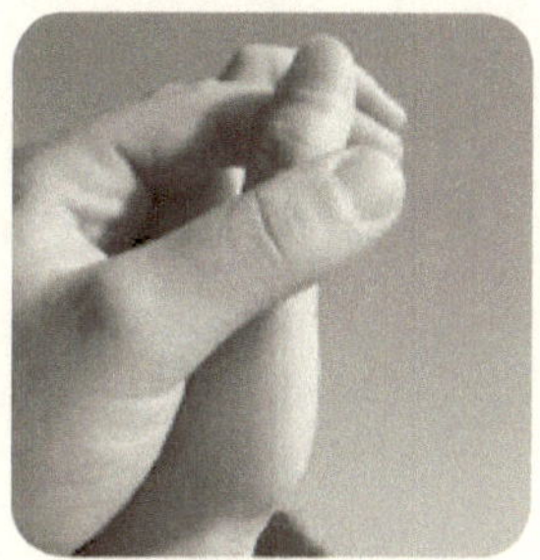

- 48 -

Angel with Fur Instead of Wings

"We live in a world of many alarms, none of which sound our true concerns."

– Guy Mankowski

Singer, psychologist and author Guy Mankowski, sums up our life today in a sentence. Although we have more time and money than ever before, most of us have little sense of control over our own lives. The pace is hectic and we are slaves to a routine that we believe helps us make sense of our day to day. Even if there is small change in the schedule life becomes a centrifuge and we are flung in different directions. A mind so conditioned by schedules, high in stress and light on substance gives little opportunity to think critically, and even less chance to experience life meaningfully by being in the present moment.

I am talking about life today in general and my life in particular. Both my husband and I have stressful jobs and a teenager and a pre -teen at home. Life is hectic, busy and even a small incident like the driver coming in late has us on the hop. Imagine our surprise…shock rather when our elder daughter asked us for a puppy as a birthday present. Did she have any idea how this would throws our precariously balanced routine out of control? We tried to dissuade her and counselled her against the pitfalls, however, the tenacity of the teenager won and we bowed down to what fate had in store for us.

'Prince' our golden retriever came home in July. It's only been a little over 3 months and already our lives are transformed…and in a good way! It's not just that all of us find time to be with the pup to bask in his unconditional love but also how we all have learned to care about something beyond ourselves. We have learnt to take it slow and sit with Prince and pet him. His vitality, joy at the smallest of things and his appreciation of life is something that has taught us as a family to be grateful for all that we have and relish the simple pleasures that life can bring. We all laugh together at his antics, are touched by his 'puppy eyes' and ignore the mess he sometimes creates. My daughters have learnt to be more responsible and grounded. We discuss his diet, buy him toys, talk about his pranks and are connected through his love. He has taught us all to be less selfish, more giving and best of all to live in the moment. The deadlines haven't disappeared, they are just a little fuzzy and have lost their bite.

I am coming to realise that no matter how close we are to another person, few human relationships are as free from conflict, expectations and disillusionment as is the relationship you have with a dog. Few of us can give of themselves to another as a dog gives of itself. Pets they say are our seat belts on the emotional roller coaster of life--they can be trusted, they keep us safe, and they sure do smooth out the ride. Their untainted souls knowingly or unknowingly make us wish - that we were as innocent as they are, and make us ache for a place where innocence is universal and where the meanness, the betrayals, and the cruelties of this world are unknown.

We all have found our small utopia (it will keep growing), our escape from the realities, disappointments and constant demands of life. It's called 'Prince'.

Pura Vida!

Catchphrases come and go, but it is truly rare for them to find a place outside the confining boundaries of cultures from which they are born. A Mexican movie, entitled "Pura Vida," captured people's imagination in Costa Rica. Locals thought the phrase underscored their idyllic lifestyle. They began to ardently use it to express positive feelings about anyone or anything. The catchword Pura Vida could mean any of the following. 'Pure life', 'take it easy', 'enjoy life' 'all good' and 'this is life'. This phrase made boundaries invisible as it percolated into the western United States and Central America as an unassuming, succinct way to describe a person or place that radiates simple joy.

All the different connotations and meanings of this phrase draw our attention to the fact that a pure life is good, simple, easy and elemental. We rob the simplicity (joyfulness) from our life by making it complex or adulterated. Life is play between need and responsibility. Lower your need and the responsibility decreases. Once responsibility decreases we fret less and can focus on the essentials.

A man works ungodly hours, puts in a lot of hard-work, and undergoes incredible stress to be able to afford a holiday to an exotic foreign location. While he is meeting the last-minute deadlines, he inadvertently exchanges harsh words with a colleague and leaves his workplace in a huff. He stops at a park and sees a man dressed like a monk reading under a tree. The monk is unkempt, however seems so blissful and unaware of his surrounding that the man is intrigued. After questioning he finds out that the shabby man is quite educated and well read. He does odd and end jobs to meet his needs. Since the conversation is stimulating the man offers his business card to the man under the tree. Just a few days later, the monk from the park comes to see the man in his office. His dishevelled appearance causes some speculation, however, it soon subsides as everyone is busy. The man tells the monk that he is educated, intelligent and must do something worthwhile with his life. The monk makes himself at home and asks, "Like how?" The man promises a job to him in his company: "It would be long hours, some stress and hard-work. But, you will be well compensated and rewarded". Again, the monk's question remains the same. "Like how?" The man gets slightly annoyed: "What do you mean like how? You will have a steady income, respect and occasionally like me you can fulfil your musings by visiting your dream destination". "What will you do in your dream destination?" asks the monk. "I'll relax, connect with nature and catch up on what I really love to do" replies the man.

The monk smiled and said "What do you think I was doing when you first met me at the park? When I can do all the things you mentioned effortlessly, why should I take up this demanding job?"

The man had nothing to say.

What you are seeking might just be found in a park in your vicinity. Simplicity has its own rewards. Going back to catchphrase, keep it simple, take it easy and Pura Vida!

- 50 -

Question the Question

My family has a love and hate relationship with Mathematics. I dislike it, however, my husband and daughters show great affinity towards it. My younger daughter got a rather complex question in math as homework. She attempted to resolve it, however, the answer seemed elusive and beyond her reach. I asked my elder daughter to explain the problem to her. She however, did not resolve the dilemma, in fact she did nothing to work out a solution. She encouraged the little one to ask a series of questions to clarify her doubts pertaining to the question (a teaching style, learnt from their father). At some point their father chipped in and then began another barrage of questions. I was wondering how the little one could come up with one question after another and if her query was being resolved in the process, when unexpectedly it seemed her doubts were cleared and she went to her room to write her response.

I didn't quite understand what had transpired when my husband explained the situation with a little anecdote. A psychiatrist, who was used to prescribing medications, and spending time with patients on prescription management found solace and comfort in scientific and logical transactions. Mysticism and ingenuousness was lost on him. When he met a Zen monk he saw this as a chance to clarify a doubt he had been carrying in his mind for a very long time. Seeing the Monk receptive, the psychiatrist asked "How exactly do you help people with their mental anguish? What technique do you use?" The monk laughed. "I have no technique, no answers. I don't even deliberately help them. I just get them to a point where they don't feel the need to ask any more questions, from me or from life". "How does this work?" asked the baffled psychiatrist. "It's simple said the monk, the answer lies within each one of us. We just need to remove the layers of doubts one by one." The psychiatrist smiled, swept for a moment by the mysteries of the mind.

By questioning our own questions, our own truths we begin a journey that goes back to remove the barriers that we might have created in our own learning path. This seemingly regressive journey actually propels us forward as it unearths the answers that lie within us all along. My daughter found the answer when she exhausted her questions. Once the ripples run their course, the water is calm again. In this clear water pearls of wisdom reveal themselves.

- 51 -

Seeing Beyond Exteriors

Many of the truths we cling to depend greatly on our point of view. How we perceive things is more a reflection of our soul and who we are as people rather that how things actually are. At some point it become important to see distant things as if they were close and to see things that are close with some distance. We then might attain an overall picture that is occasionally lost due to our narrow perceptions. Here is a contemporary story that underscores the fact that heightened discernment should be our goal -becoming more aware of how we see, not just what we see.

A young man in his early twenties looked outside the window of the train compartment and ecstatically exclaimed; "Dad look how the trees are moving backwards". The father smiles in agreement as the other people sitting in the compartment look confused. Soon the young man exclaims again "Dad look a tunnel is approaching…I'm so excited to see how getting in and out of the tunnel will look like". The father continues to smile and says "wait and watch". As they come out of the tunnel the confusion in the faces of men seated in the same compartment had changed to pity. "You must show your poor chap to a good psychiatrist or doctor" one of them said.

The father responded. "We are just returning from our visit to the hospital. Only today my son's bandages have been removed. He was born blind, however, a kind organ donor has changed his life. He is able to see for the first time today. I can't help but share his excitement as he is seeing things that he has never seen before."

The entire compartment was silent. The smirks and pitiful smiles vanished. How quickly everyone had jumped to conclusions not realizing that the truth is not only paradoxical but also surprising. Before we rush to make judgments we must consider that our tunnel vision is the biggest impediment to knowing the truth. Rumi says; "Be the melting snow. Wash yourself of yourself". We must come out of the proverbial dark tunnel free of our biases, prejudices and limitations. In the ensuing light the beauty of the truth will be revealed.

52

Simple Living

I have often encouraged my parents to buy new things, things that I thought would simplify their lives and make it more comfortable. It's only after vising them that I realized that simplicity is about taking away the excess, and keeping the meaningful.

After a long time, I visited my parents and my childhood home. There was something about the rather old edifice that not only embraced like home but also exuded and aura of tranquility.

Every room was not only reminiscent of our growing years but also had at least one object that had endured the test of time and become more valuable with each passing year. My father proudly talked about a fan that fascinatingly spun in the veranda. "We bought it when we got married and it's never given us trouble since. Just a bit of gentle cleaning is all it needs" he said gazing at the fan almost affectionately.

In another room sat two chairs which had definitely seen better days, but were still quite comfortable and comforting. It was evident that they had been well looked after. Our history had seeped into the crevices and so had a little bit of love. "These chairs are older than you" he said looking at the chairs as my mother smiled indulgently.

Similar objects adorned every room. A bookrack whose hinges creaked a little and a small stool with a weak leg that needed extra attention when dislodged. My parents valued everything that they owned and had taken care of things such that they rarely felt the need to acquire new things. Every object in the home served a purpose and it served the purpose well.

This minimalistic lifestyle of my parents is perhaps one of the reasons why serenity pervaded every part of the house. The deliberate promotion of the things they valued and acquiring only what they needed drove home the point of simple living. It requires a conscious decision, gratitude, affinity towards the resources natural and otherwise and a deep sense of contentment to not succumb to the culture of overconsumption.

If we learn to be content; take care of what we have; rejoice in the way things are, then we will realize that there is nothing lacking and that the whole world belongs to us.

53

Simple Yet Significant

Recently three funny, simple yet significant encounters with children presented me with a fresh uncomplicated perspective towards life. While going for a walk one evening I noticed a little boy pulling up on his toes, trying to reach a door bell. I decided to give him a helping hand…and rang the bell for him. Imagine my shock when the bugger turned around and ran saying; "Thanks Aunty…now…run". The scowl of the grumpy old man who answered the door did nothing to mitigate my embarrassment. Later, I did however, find myself smiling at my own gullibility and pragmatism.

My second interaction was with a little girl who was walking alongside her mother; an acquaintance of mine. Both mother and child were pushing their own prams. I spoke to the new mother about the baby and thinking that that the little girl would feel ignored, I bent down to her pram and politely looked at the doll she had placed there. "Oh! how lovely…is this your baby?" I asked. "No!" she exclaimed with some derision and looked at me curiously. "This is my doll" she said. When I stared at her stupefied she kindly explained "They are a lot less trouble than babies". My eyes met her mother's and both of us smiled in agreement.

For the third interaction I didn't have to go too far. My younger daughter was taking her own sweet time over her favourite book and snack while I fretted over her homework not being complete. I pulled her up and gave her a talk about all that I did around the house when I was her age. I spoke to her about responsibility and time management while she sat there unimpressed. As soon as I finished speaking she said; "What about fun Ma? Just because you didn't have fun during your childhood, doesn't mean that I don't get to enjoy myself either". I knew she was being cheeky and yet words deserted me and despite myself I smiled.

As we mature into adults we forget our childlike ability to have fun, to speak our mind and to take life at face value. We become cautious, look for hidden agendas and value the politically correct over truth. We use euphemisms, polite conversations and reason to tide over situations that wouldn't be so complicated in the first place if we had kept things simple. Children don't see the world as complicated as we adults do. They forgive easily and quickly, they dream, they explore, they believe and best of all; they dust themselves after a fall and run again. They usually find magic because they go out looking for it.

We adults must bottle their childlike enthusiasm, simplicity, candour and cheer and carry this potion in our practical pockets at all times. Whenever, things get too heavy, or twisted or dry…all we need to do is open this bottle and let the potion do its magic.

- 54 -

Stairway to Heaven

German Lyric poet Friedrich Holderlin has so rightly said "*What has always made a hell on Earth has been that man has tried to make it his heaven*". Earth will have its own trials and tribulations, and the only way to bliss is in creating one's heaven on earth by leaving behind our self-regarding ways.

Sin makes its own hell and goodness its own heaven. While explaining this notion and the symbolic key difference between heaven and hell a professor once drew up two scenarios in front of his students. Scenario one comprised of some hungry people and a huge pot of delicious food. However, what prevented them from enjoying this succulent dish, was the fact that they were given extremely long spoons to eat the food. The spoons were too long and each person remained hungry as they wrought all possible permutations but were unable to get the spoon anywhere near their deprived mouths. Strife and pain was evident. The men were all miserable, angry and hungry. "Looks pretty much like hell Eh?" says the professor.

Scenario two was similar yet different. The hungry men, long spoons and the simmering pot of food remained the same. The differences came from the fact that people quickly realized that they cannot feed themselves given the length of the spoons. Instead of trying all possible ways of feeding themselves they decided it makes more sense to feed each other. The length of the spoons was no longer an impediment in assuaging hunger as each man was fed by another in their group. Tranquillity and love reigned. Resultant: The men were satiated, happy and peaceful. Sounds quite like heaven.

Therefore, one may deduct that when man slogs only to make his own heaven (feeding himself with the long spoon) he is not only unsuccessful in doing so but instead paves way to hell due to his acute self-centredness. Whereas, when a man tries to make heaven for others (feeding someone else with the long spoon), he not only brings satiation to another soul but also overlays a road to heaven for himself.

It is our grit and resilience and helps us humans to manipulate our circumstances and find or create meaning even in grim and depraved situations.

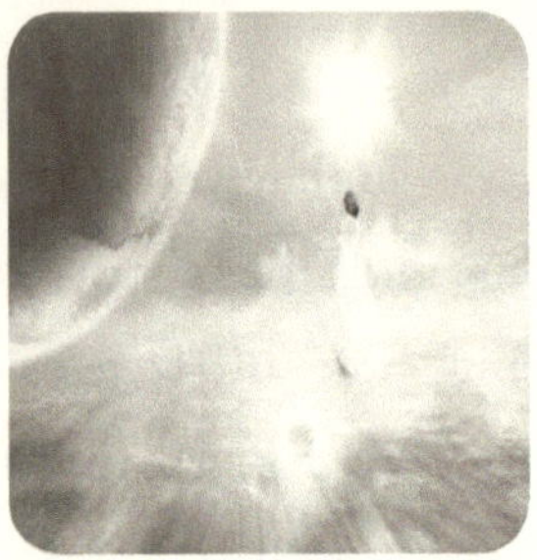

55

Stop Reacting. Start Responding

Our work places are becoming increasingly hostile. In our attempt at meeting deadlines, combating stress and climbing the career ladder, interpersonal relationships, regard and affection are often compromised. In the heat of the moment one does not realise that harsh criticism can truly hurt and relationships that take years to build can be shattered in a moment. Since e-mails are the order of the day; they further mitigate the connection between individuals and one is lost is a conundrum of words that confuse more than they explain. The by products are hurt and angst that renders us volatile in the face of criticism. We react negatively and the resultant is degeneration of emotional well -being and ultimately relationships. We cannot control the criticism that comes to us, luckily, we are bequeathed with the gifts of self-control, self-awareness and cognitive fecundity. Collectively, they give us the freedom to shape, respond and eventually change how negative criticism impacts us.

Self- control is essential as it gives us the precious grip on time and the ability to respond instead of react to a particular situation. If we just take a step backward when faced with criticism we will find we are better able to cope with it. Self- awareness comes in as a close second. Our thought patterns, emotions, intuitions or gut feelings become more pronounced and as we navigate this internal process. We come to an objective and clearer understanding; either the criticism was deserved or that the criticism was unfair and came from an unmerited source. In both cases a confrontation will not help. Lastly, our cognitive fecundity will tell us; if the criticism was deserved, instead of retaliating we must learn from it. In the other eventuality that the criticism and source was unfair; there is little point in contesting it. Prodding and poking will only make matters worse and rob you of your happiness, instead walk away quietly and with a clear conscience.

Circumstances will ride you if you let them, instead, buy time, regulate your thought process and move from reactive to proactive thinking. It is always better to conquer yourself than to win over others. Anyone can criticise, but it takes someone wise, someone with character and resolve to separate the chaff from grain and move on.

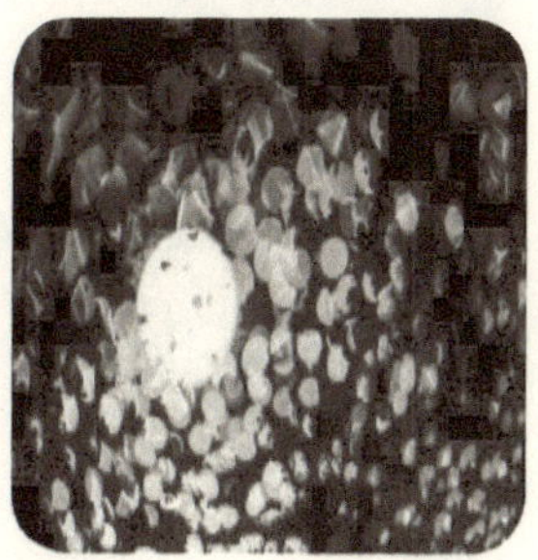

56

Take Care of Yourself

We are all a part of a volatile, uncertain and complex world that demands long hours, quick resolutions and instant gratification. In meeting the demands of time and circumstances the cumulative result is such that more often than not we forget to nurture ourselves. It is no wonder that in every plane ride we are reminded that in case of emergencies we are supposed to help ourselves first and then proceed to help others.

Here is a parable that brings this message home to us. There were once three acrobats. These entertainers performed each day on the streets in order to earn a living. Their life depended on precision and balance. Their act consisted of two of them balancing on the opposite ends of a bamboo pole. The pole would be positioned on the shoulder of the third acrobat.

All three performers had to maintain complete focus and balance in order to prevent any mishaps. The station of the two performers on top was particularly precarious as they had to maintain equilibrium while understanding the stance of the other. Although they had honed their skill to perfection, yet each day as they got on to the pole they felt tremors of apprehension. Naturally, they wanted to mitigate this anxiety. "Let's watch out for each other, so that we can help each other maintain concentration and balance. You measure the steps I take and position yourself accordingly" said one.

Just as the second acrobat nodded his head is acquiescence, the third acrobat, the wise acrobat who had been listening to their conversation spoke; "I think it would be best if both of you examined yourself. To look after oneself means to look after all of us. It has worked so far and I don't see any reason why it should not work in future. If each of us are mindful of what we need to do, our act will take care of itself".

By taking care of yourself, by learning to nourish your mind and body you organically begin to treat those around you with more consideration, love and benevolence. Hence, you naturally create a positive impact around you. All humans have the ability to love.

It must begin with loving yourself and the equilibrium of life will take care of itself.

- 57 -

The Art of Gifting

I've always believed that gifting in an art that few have mastered…and I've counted myself among the chosen few who are well into mastering it. I plan carefully before an event, consider the likes, dislikes and taste of the person and then go out of my way to 'emerge' with the perfect gift. People I know think I'm wonderful when it comes to giving the perfect gifts and I almost believed them until I learnt from experience that gifting is not really an art but a simple act of finding the best time to give what one needs rather than what one wants.

I admit, albeit grudgingly, that this lesson was taught to me by my husband who rarely, if at all engages in buying presents. Recently, he gave me two gifts which not only made me reconsider my own passion for gifting but also opened my world to new perspectives and thoughts. My involvement with what I received has made me experience and see the world a little differently.

With two kids, a full -time job and other tasks that I had taken upon myself; life was rather stressful. I barely had any time for myself and was running from the axiomatic pillar to post. The ramifications soon became evident in the form of health concerns. Very timely, my husband enrolled us in 'The Art of living course'. Initially, I was bogged down by the logistics, however, I accepted his gift. What I heard during the course was routine, however what I experienced was something totally different. To think of nothing else for the next three days except where my life was going 'spiritually' was an experience that I had not luxuriated in before. In the subsequent days, I comprehended the need to exert the power of will and control my mind to reflect upon its actions and their ramifications. I didn't come out of the course a changed person, I did however, see myself standing at the beginning of a path that I had not explored before. What made it more enticing was the fact that the path was uncomplicated and the terrain simple. I just had to walk the mile and find emotional and mental sustenance.

The second gift was equally unexpected. On our 20th Anniversary people hinted that I should expect 'a huge rock' or other expensive jewellery-something I truly don't care about. My husband surprised me…which I thought was an accomplishment after 20 years of marriage! He got me a radio! It could play more than 5000 songs depending on my mood at any given moment. Music has always been my love and passion and a radio meant childhood, youth, nostalgia, music and love all rolled into one. I was thrilled that he knew what I needed and what would genuinely make me happy. It wouldn't be an exaggeration to say that I carry the radio everywhere inside our home.

I have come to understand that giving/gifting is simple when we give with love. Gifts need no frills, no lace and no wrapping paper. It is not an art to be mastered; it is a simple act which connects one heart with the other.

- 58 -

The Art of Giving

"Deeds of giving are the very foundations of the world"

– Jewish saying

Come December, the school I teach in is abuzz with activity. For a few weeks before Christmas we play the game 'Secret Santa'. The game goes like this. The names of all the players are written down in strips of paper and put in a bowl. Each of us goes and pics a chit. The person whose name we pick becomes our 'buddy' and we become his /her secret Santa. In the ensuing weeks leading to Christmas we covertly send little notes and gifts to brighten the day of our buddy. Everyone gets creative and thinks of ways of making their buddy happy. As you can imagine, there is an air of festivity and joy in the school. Also, an air of mystery I might add, as each one tries to guess who his or her Santa is. The event culminates in a Christmas party where amid great laughter and surprise the identity of the Santa is finally revealed.

This entrenched event sees so many people going out of their way to make the season a joyous one for others. Some write little notes of love and affection while others go and buy the cutest and sweetest presents for their buddy. The season is such…even the shops and malls are replete with gift hampers and the scent of giving permeates the air.

It is very interesting to observe, how in most cultures festivals are inexplicably intertwined with giving gifts. Benevolent acts add to our joy and celebration as they not only celebrate the occasion/festival but also the human spirit. There is nothing like seeing a smile spread over a face as a gift is unravelled. The act, let's say art of giving comes from the same place inside you from where stems your deepest happiness. Hence it resonates with such contentment, warmth and joy that it rejuvenates both – the giver and the one who receives.

With Christmas around the corner spreading joyfulness through philanthropic acts will again gain impetus and if you missed out this Diwali then here is chance for you to make up. In a world that is increasingly getting selfish, a moment set aside to think of someone else will do no harm. These 'giving' exchanges promote a sense of trust and cooperation that strengthens our ties to others.

Having positive social interactions, like in the game I mentioned above, fosters a heightened sense of interdependence and solidarity in our school community. What's more, when we give to others, we don't only make them feel closer to us; we also feel closer to them. Whether you're on the giving or receiving end of a gift, that gift can elicit feelings of gratitude—it can be a way of expressing gratitude or instilling gratitude in the recipient. Giving then leads to a win win situation.

Charles W. Howard says it best- "they err who think Santa Claus enters through the chimney. He enters through the heart."

The Avengers!

Here is an interesting episode that forced me to consider how sometimes joy can be found in not only unexpected but rather trying situations.

Avengers End Game finally dawned on the skies of Bangalore, and my children were extremely animated to see the movie. What I didn't realize is that every other child in Bangalore was also just as enthusiastic. We soon found out that the cinemas were all booked. We tried almost all we had in the vicinity and were disappointed. It seemed that the peace and quiet of my household would come to an end if I didn't find a way to show my kids the alleged last movie of the avengers.

As always, my husband came to the rescue. He found the tickets in a 'local cinema hall' not far from our home in the suburbs. Now, the kids were not sure whether they should continue to be excited about it or not...as they would eventually get to watch the movie, however, it would not be in the sanitized, luxurious environment of a mall and it certainly wouldn't be 'gold class'. However, the tug of the movie was strong and we found ourselves in front of the 'local cinema' unable to park our car. The crowd was intense and the weather sultry. As always in India, there was some order in the disorder and at some point we were able to park our car. Now, we only had to face the queue… wait there was no queue. There were just people who seemed to have cornered the cinema hall from all sides and their tribe kept increasing. Being used to the clinical but comfortable environment of the mall, I was the first to complain and my children fast followed suit. It took, jostling, wriggling of the nose and forever to finally get inside the theatre. Finally fans! …wait …were their no ACs?

As we sat in the not so comfortable seats, we were prepared to be disappointed. The cardboard 3D glasses we got did nothing to reassure us. The first few scenes of the movie were a blur literally and figuratively as we adjusted to the environment, seats and the glasses. Finally the pace picked up. As a super hero entered the screen there was loud whistling and cheering from the audience despite the fact that the dialogues were almost lost in the din. Dismayed we trudged along. At some point we got engrossed and the screaming did not bother us; we might have shrieked along a few times. In the climactic scene (battle between Thanos and the Avengers) everyone shouted and whistled.

We were amazed to find ourselves amongst the ones cheering and hooting. We had found self-expression! We were as loud (if not louder) than everyone else. We completely enjoyed ourselves. The entire theatre notwithstanding the shabby surroundings came to support a common cause-the Avengers.

We came out of the movie theater thrilled and on a high note. It felt we were a part of the film. We might have even smiled at the strangers (who we had pushed earlier). Our screams had reduced half the dialogues to dust but we did not care. We did not care that it took forever (again!) to come out of the parking lot and that everything was unorganized. In the same high note we drove home.

What I realized then is that our clinical lives might not have a lot to offer us in terms of excitement and joy. However, once in a while if we experiment with life, it might just surprise us.

60

The Best Journey Takes You Home

The prospect of going home is very appealing. What makes it even more appealing is the fact that there is someone waiting for you at home. That someone could be a parent, a spouse, a child or a friend and often due to the hectic pace of our life this special someone is taken for granted. Here is a pintsized fable that puts the spotlight back on the person who makes the home a sanctuary.

While chasing a cow the lion and the cow both fall in quicksand. The lion, used to manipulating a situation in his favor took some time to realize that this condition was beyond his control. Out of habit, however, he kept growling and trying to push himself out of the swamp. He even made threatening moves towards the cow. The cow on the other hand was calm and seemingly unperturbed. This further disconcerted the lion. He said, "Don't you know we are going to die? Are you delusional? Like the ostrich are you also pretending that the situation does not exist?"

The cow smiled at the lion's agitation. She said "I am quiet and composed because I am certain I will be saved". The lion was further unnerved. The cow went on to explain. "I have a master. When I don't reach home before night fall, he will come looking for me. He will pull me out of this distress." The lion scoffed at this. However, as if on cue, at twilight a few men came towards the quicksand. One of them saw the plight of the cow and made arrangements to pull her out. And as the sun disappeared from the horizon the lion saw the cow going home with her master.

Having someone who literally and figuratively waits for our safe return, not only makes us more confident and poised individuals, but also makes our home and eventually our heart a sanctuary. And if, we do get caught in the quicksand of our thoughts and actions this sanctuary will not only offer us a branch out of the quagmire, but will also burn bright and illuminate our heart. And if there is light in our heart we will certainly find our way back home.

61

God's Plan

A disciple seemed particularly perturbed by what has recently transpired in his life. The hurt seemed to be corroding his very soul. When despite the passage of time he still seemed preoccupied with his distress the master appeared. "What is it that has cast this shadow in your heart and mind"? The master asked. "I am dejected with life; nothing seems to be going well" replied the disciple. The master smiled. "Are you sure nothing is going well? Is the cosmos, the moon and the stars moving in alignment"? He asked.

"Yes" whispered the confused disciple.

"Is the sun rising in the east and setting in the west? Is the earth rotating as per plan in its axis?"

"Yes", said the disciple again.

Is the moon following its lunar cycle? Do the tides still come in and retreat from the shores of the ocean?

The disciple nodded in acquiescence.

The master continued relentlessly. "Did the sun rise today morning? Are you certain it will set at night? Are the seasons in alignment with the natural order?

The disciple could only answer in affirmative.

"Then what is it that concerns you this deeply? What is the thought that is scattering the galaxies, stopping the earth from rotation, disrupting the seasons and dismantling the sun for you? Your lack of perspective is obvious when you let a little nasty thought in your mind dissolve all the good that's happening around you and possibly to you. When everything is going according to God's plan you cannot be excluded from it"

The disciple hung his head; how insignificant his concern seemed now when compared to the schema of sun, ocean and tides. He understood that in the larger design of things little hurts, tiny bursts of anger or grief are insignificant bubbles that should be left to dissipate in the thin air.

Seeing the disciple receptive the master continued "Be like the water; graceful, supple, soft and subtly prevailing. Once you are like water; you will find your way despite the obstacles in your path"

It was as though his masters parting words had sanctified him and the elements. He felt as light as air. The sun illuminated the corners of his mind. The water gently cleansed his heart and the sway of the tides lulled his soul to peace.

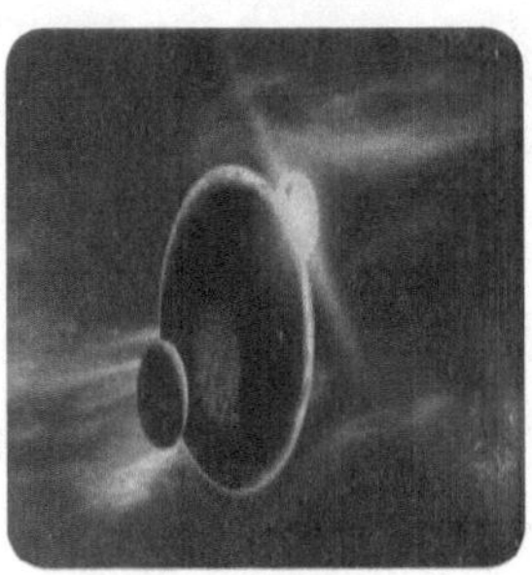

62

The Bigger Picture

Recently, a friend of mine forwarded an old post on the much publicized Pulitzer award winning picture. Called 'The vulture and the little girl' the photograph was praised for how forcefully and emotionally it captured the human suffering in South Sudan. No written narrative of the famine could make so striking a point as this single picture.

What is thought-provoking however, is what actually transpired in the life of Kevin Carter after he won this prestigious award. The celebration was short-lived as the strain he was experiencing from a career of photographing horrific situations was compounded by a question asked by an astute journalist. "What did you do to help the girl"? Kevin could not answer this question satisfactorily and the journalist summed up the perceived lack of empathy in one powerful statement. "There were two vultures that day; and one of them had a camera".

Empathy is the chief source of energy that can connect one human being to another, touch a heart and give a psychological hug when one needs it the most. We could be erudite scientists, engineers, teachers and photographers as in this case, however, without empathy we fail as humans. Being compassionate makes us humane and being humane makes us understand human misery and work towards mitigating it.

The photograph and the hullabaloo surrounding it were added stress in a life spent capturing atrocities on camera. Winning an award for one such poignant image only added to the culpability Carter probably felt; he buckled under the pressure and took his own life. Arguably, there was probably little he could have done to help the girl, but did he do that little? It then becomes easy to judge someone who watched and took photographs while a human being suffered.

Technology has made taking and sharing pictures and videos of human shame and suffering, easy, however, our focus must be to take steps to lighten it. What makes us different from the other species is to be mindful and act on our empathetic impulses. Instead of taking his own life, if carter had channeled his grief and understanding in a direction that could help alleviate someone else's pain the legacy he would have left behind would have been altogether different.

- 63 -

The 'C' Word

"Cancer is a word, not a sentence."

– Rob Buckman

John Diamon might have enunciated the above-mentioned quote, however, I know of someone who has not only exemplified the attitude this quote proliferates but also inspired me with her grit and resilience. Her indomitable spirit left me contemplating on how pain and hardships need not be weights that pull us down but can be fuel for the journey we call life.

My hands shook, voice quivered and my mind went on an over drive as Ms. Benjamin, my friend of more than 15 years told me she had cancer. Cancer at any age is petrifying, however, cancer when you are at the wrong side of 70 is like reaching the end of the rope without having a knot there to hold on to. I just didn't know what to say, or how to be her solace. As I groped for the right words, there was a sudden role reversal and it was she who gave me not only solace but also wisdom that only the chosen few who've found courage in unlikely places can give.

She talked of her chemo sessions as though they were just a tough round of physical exercise. She talked about her fears as though they were a prerequisite to hope and philosophized her pain to an extent that it felt like panacea. All this time I thought to myself if there is ever a lesson to learn in life- it is now. Here I was, all ready with some empathy and a lot of sympathy to offer to my elderly friend, instead, I found myself picking pearls of wisdom that she gave away with such abandon. It was as if this difficult point in her life had heightened her understanding and perception of things that really matter. Sharing photographs, poetry, quotes, letters, songs and other everyday things took on a different dimension and she could seek and find meaning in the mundane. All I did was emotionally and mentally stand beside her and soak it all in.

My friend is slowly recovering and yes, her family and friends have played a huge role in pulling her up, however, like most meaningful fights this is the fight with self. This is the fight of not letting debilitating situations beat you. Sandy Fussell, children's author, freelance writer says "Life is all about balance. Since I have only one leg, I understand that well."

Everything can be taken away from us, our circumstances can be the most extenuating, however, what we can still retain is the attitude with which we deal with these situations. Our conditions do not make or break a person they just reveal him. When a storm is raging around us, we can and should hold on to faith, to hope, to friends, to family and to love with both our hands. And once the tempest has passed we will find in our hands remnants of things that truly matter.

And as my friend says "Cancer may have started the fight, but I will finish it." - I believe her.

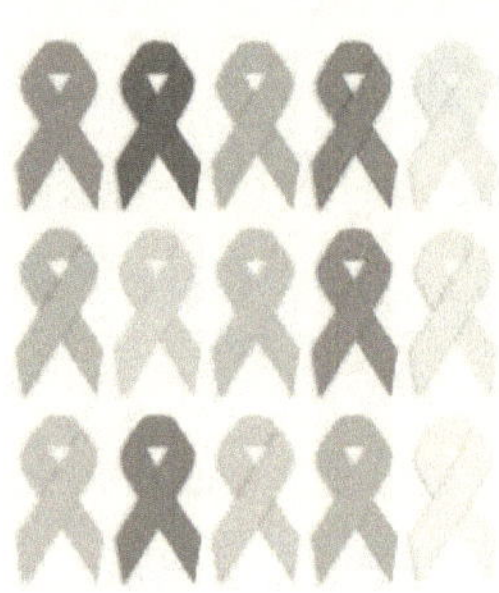

- 64 -

The Greatest Challenge

The only way to improve is by little and large victories over ourselves. The true contest is when you battle with your mind and you win.

Two childhood friends met after years of separation. Both were now young adults having disparate views on life. One had become a monk and the other was a skilled archer. The young archer was rather boastful. "I have attained great dexterity is controlling the arrow and so far I have not missed a single target. Have you acquired any such skill"? He taunted. "I am trying to acquire some skill at controlling my mind" said the young monk sagaciously. "What good is that?" said the archer to his friend as he demonstrated remarkable expertise when he hit a bull's eye on his first try, and then as if to prove a point split that arrow with his second shot.

"Can you match that!" he tested. Unperturbed, the young monk did not even touch the bow. Instead, he beckoned the young archer to follow him up the mountain. Curious and assuming that he had made his friend self-conscious the archer followed him high into the mountain until they reached a deep crevasse bridged by a rather fragile and rickety log. Serenely stepping out onto the middle of the tottering and hazardous bridge, the young monk picked a difficult target, drew his bow, and achieved a clean, direct hit. "Now it is your turn," he said as he graciously stepped back onto the safe ground. Regarding with terror the seemingly bottomless and precarious abyss, the young man could not direct himself to even approach the log, no less shoot at a target. "You have great skill with your bow," said the monk intuiting his friend's dilemma, "but you have little skill with the mind that fires the shot. Once you learn to control your mind you can control everything."

The archer now looked bashful yet transformed. "Thank you" was all he said.

There is little or no point in controlling the entire world when you can't control your own mind. Yes, it is an arduous, difficult test but the victory is divine. The greatest challenge is to win over your mind; to be the bow, the arrow, the log and the target all at once.

The Juggler

"Life is about balance. The good and the bad. The highs and the lows. The pina and the colada."

– Ellen DeGeneres

They say all mothers are working mothers and I agree - no matter what your circumstances or your disposition —raising children is a challenging task. There will be good days and not so good days. There will be days you bask in contentment and days you wonder how you're going to keep your head from exploding.

Now, apart from being a 'working mother' if you also have a full - time job the situation gets further challenging. The hurdles vary from having a not so spotlessly clean house to scheduling nightmares and extreme exhaustion to working mom guilt. There are moments when all of these hurdles materialize on the same day and you tell yourself; "this is impossible". And yet, you keep jumping the hurdles one by one and find that bit by bit you made the 'impossible'; 'almost possible'.

There are times when I've missed the PTA meetings, performances and mails sent by the school. There have been times when I've not sent 'home made snacks' for the class party, or thrown the best birthday party ever. I admit I've bought impulsive online gifts to tide over the fact that I wasn't where I was supposed to be. My children have probably forgiven but certainly not forgotten and I am often plagued by working mother's guilt. Is it ok to value quality as much as quantity when it comes to spending time with kids? Do my kids know that I love them as much as any other mom and that I also love my job? I keep telling myself that every family is different, and we're choosing to do what's best for ours, however sometimes this reassurance is not enough and I wonder if I'm doing it right by my children and my job. In striking a balance between the two am I underperforming in both the principal areas of my life? And every time I read articles on effective parenting and find myself struggling on the thin rope I walk sometimes; the guilt and doubt intensifies.

The reassurance, however, did come from a surprising source. During a 'Gallery walk' organized by the school

I read a well - articulated piece written by my daughter. "The Juggler" was the title. The article talked about how she admired my balancing acts both at home and work. She joked about how I had developed eyes behind my head as even while I was working on the laptop I knew what she and her sister were up to. The article concluded saying that she would try to seek a sense of balance and would not give up on things/people she loved simply because things got difficult.

It dawned on me then that I need not worry about planting my girls in neat cultivated pots; and that just like me, they will learn to bloom where they are planted even if it is the wilderness sometimes.

- 66 -

The Land of the Gods

"Great Pan is not dead;

he simply emigrated

to India.

Here, the gods roam freely,

disguised as snakes or monkeys;

every tree is sacred"

Sujata Bhatt begins her poem 'A Different History" by saying that all Gods are welcome and that several effects; even trees and animals are idolized and worshipped in India. This observation became particularly pertinent when I visited my hometown in Uttrakhand, also known as 'Dev Bhoomi'. The name literally translates to 'the land of the Gods' and rightly so as the entire locale is replete with shrines. You cannot drive for more than a few kilometers, if at all, without encountering a temple of one of the many Gods in the Hindu mythology. In fact in the particular region that I was travelling there were at least three temples of the same God within a kilometer radius.

Some of these places of worship are extremely old and of much historical and archeological value. Others have just sprung up in and around the area. The scenic locale; the deodar and pine trees and the distant mountains provided the perfect backdrop for the abodes of the Gods.

As we went from one temple to the other, my mother insisted that we sit in each spot for some time. "This is to soak in the divine energy" she stated with some persuasion. She related the fact that in India we have so many Gods and Goddesses and as many temples because all these seemingly diminutive dwellings of Gods sanctify the expanse around them. It came as no surprise that the entire province resonated with peace and tranquility. It seemed the many temples and the many Gods in them had blessed the entire region.

It is said that the heart and the mind are the true temples, however, one cannot undermine the certain degree of calm, bliss and positive energy one experiences in a sanctuary made for the Gods. Our heart feels lighter as the burdens of life disappear, leaving us spirited and alive.

All the positive vibes, hopes and aspirations combine to recognize the harmony and serenity we can find for ourselves in the mystical cocoons of our hallowed temples. I returned from the deified environs restored and cognizant of the fact that whether we visit temples of the mind or of brick and stone; they do provide a sanctuary, a repose for the heart and mind.

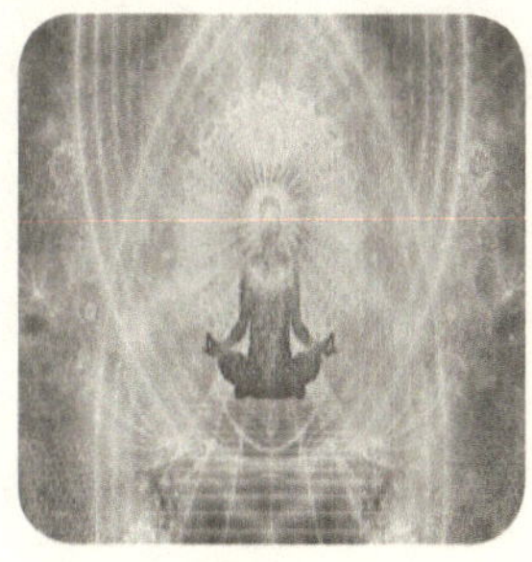

67

The Salt of the Earth

A lot of times we identify everything based on our immediate context. We don't really see the big picture for our lives and hence have a rather myopic view of situations and things. The big picture doesn't just emerge from looking from a distance; it also comes from time and expansion of our perspective.

A master, tired of his novice's complains about life and living; decided to make him see things from a different standpoint. He asked his apprentice to get a fist full of salt. When the apprentice returned, the master dictated that he put the fistful of salt in a glass of water and drink it. Looking at the novices' bitter expression the master asked "How does it taste?"

"Toxic," spit the novice.

The master only smiled and asked the novice to walk with him towards the lake. The novice although perplexed by this command said nothing and both the master and the novice walked towards the lake. "Now put the fistful of salt in the lake and then drink from the lake" said the master. As soon as the novice had taken a few sips of the water from the lake the master asked again "How does it taste now?"

"Still sweet," said the apprentice "with no taste of salt at all."

At this, the master sat beside the apprentice and said, "The momentary disappointments in life are just like salt in the lake. By concentrating only upon them and not the joys-we shrink the lake to a glass, and hence experience bitterness. You need to enlarge your scope of feeling and sense of things. Dissolve the narrow margins and understand expansive possibilities; look at the bigger picture of your life. Stop being a glass, become a lake." The apprentice smiled and the master then walked away from the lakeside.

Art they say lies in both directions –in the intricate details but also and more importantly in the broad strokes, the big picture scaffold that gives a defining shape to the artwork. And more often than not we have to watch the representation from a distance to get a better view and perspective of the painting. The understanding comes from the expansion of our viewpoint and ultimately of our heart.

68

The Secret Ingredient

Recently I came across a rather original advertisement aiming at a particular brand of tea. The advertisement started with people from different walks of life seated in separate rooms with a pot of freshly brewed tea in front of them. All of them tasted 'sample A' individually in different rooms. This I guessed, was to guarantee total attention and concentration. At the end of say 15 minutes a representative walked into their room and noted the findings. This entire process was repeated with 'sample B'. The only difference being that instead of coming after 15 minutes as in the case with sample A, this time the representative came in 5 minutes after the volunteer started drinking the tea. He/she sat along with the volunteer and had a cup of tea from the same pot. While tasting the hot brew, conversations ensued which lasted more than the time stipulated for tea tasting.

The conclusions were later shared with the entire team. An overwhelming 5 out of 6 people who tasted both the samples found that sample B tasted better. What added a rather dramatic twist to the turn of events was the revelation that both sample A and B were the same. This entire episode now begged the question; "If brand A and B were the same, how come then, five of the six volunteers had found the taste of sample B better? Was there a secret ingredient?"

The writing was clear on the wall. The secret ingredient was good company. In the first instance the volunteers drank the tea alone. In the second case the representatives came and had tea with the volunteers. This led to interesting conversations that transcended the boundaries of time and space. The tea tasted better because there was someone to share it with.

They say tea is liquid wisdom. When shared, this wisdom could lend itself to the quiet contemplation of life where things seem better and mellow. Having tea with someone then becomes an indoor picnic, a rejuvenation of sorts. It's not about the tea, it's about making time to be around people who make you feel good, make you laugh, and remind you what's important in life. When there are good people, good conversations and perhaps some tea, life tastes better.

69

The Seeker and the Sought

Even a small story can make the heart larger. Stories makes one visit places inside and outside the mind that one never knew existed. Often, they haunt and if you probe long and deep enough you find a new perspective that might have escaped you despite having heard the story several times.

One such story goes like this. A sage was sitting under a tree from where he could see the courtyard of a house in the vicinity. A child's laughter drew his attention; he saw a child running around the courtyard trying to catch his shadow as his mother watched indulgently. The child's frantic attempts to catch his shadow and mirth as the shadow escaped him brought a smile to the sage's face. No one can remain untouched by the innocence and gay abandon of a child. Soon however, the mirth faded as the child grew increasingly frustrated at not being able to catch his shadow. The mother's attempts to help were futile; and soon the child broke down in tears. The sage who had enjoyed the child's happiness could not remain unscathed by his sorrow. He got up from under the tree and walked into the courtyard of the house.

He gently asked the child to put his hands on his own head and said: "Go catch your shadow. I'm positive you will capture it this time." Emboldened by the words of the sage the child tried once again and much to his delight he found that he was holding his shadow by the head. The mother smiled gratefully at the sage as he walked back to his place under the tree.

This little story is much larger in scope and dimension. We need to first get a grip of ourselves, if we are to have a grip over what we seek. The only way to control or manipulate the external is internal. A musk deer has the fragrance within and yet runs throughout the forest trying to find it. Unlike the child and deer, we need to stop running around, pause and look inside for the answers we seek. Rumi said, "What you seek is seeking you"; and at some point, you'll find that the seeker and the sought will become one.

70

The Sheltering Tree

Every day as I go to work, I'm grateful for living and working in the suburbs. The uncluttered, traffic free drive and the verdant green landscape dotted with trees, shrubs and bushes is a delight to the senses. Words cannot fathom or express the harmony that this sight brings to the mind and no matter how the day turns out I know I've got the best start to the morning.

Imagine my shock, when on one such drive to work, I saw the huge trees that fringed the way being chopped off to broaden the road and facilitate traffic. I wondered if anyone gave a second thought to not only the deed they were so mercilessly executing but also to the ramifications of such a cruel act. A lot had been spoken about the divinity, wisdom and benefits of tress but we also need to reconsider our symbiotic relationship with them. At any given point, what they breathe out is what we breathe in and what we exhale they inhale. This is a relationship that surmounts and surpasses every other facet of life. We are because we breathe. And if it is breath that keeps us alive it wouldn't be a gross assumption to make that it is our synergetic relationships with trees that breathes life into everything we do. We are partners in the dance of life.

The seasons of life and time are so wonderfully choreographed by the trees. The tentative blossom of spring elucidates rebirth and hope. The blazing bloom of summer underscores the paradoxes of sun and shade. The learned russet of autumn talks of maturity and letting go. The hush of winter beckons rest and the need to find peace. Trees are the most powerful teachers as they communicate simply by finding roots in tough terrains, growing despite the struggle and standing tall in debilitating circumstances.

Nothing is more hallowed, more sagacious or more archetypal of beauty than a strong tree. When a tree is cut, the wound, exposes not only the rings of its years, its blemishes, all the struggle, all the anguish, all the sickness, all the pleasure and prosperity but also the ruthlessness and selfishness of man. When we fail to understand our symbiotic connection with trees we let go of this sheltering breath of life.

71

The Voice That Doesn't Use Words

Intuition they say is a direct message from your soul. More often than not we try to realize with our minds, try to make sense of the things around us with logic, however, mind is prejudiced and logic is controlled by numbers and facts. We need to use our intuition sometimes to direct our mind in the right direction.

Many argue that since we continue to evolve in complex ways we cannot depend on intuition alone. I agree to some extent, however, the more compound our world gets the more irrational it seems. And since our day-to-day social decisions have no cogent solution; we have only our intuitions to guide us.

I learnt the importance of not ignoring one's subconscious state by a sad event that recently transpired in my family. My mother is particularly fond of her oldest brother. At one point when he was very ill she almost cancelled her trip abroad to be with him. However, my uncle recovered and my mother continued with her trip. As life would have it, 2 days after she returned home from her travel she felt an instinctive urgency to go meet her brother. It was rather late in the evening and the logistics didn't quite add up. She decided to go meet him the next day. That night my uncle passed away. What made this sad occurrence particularly poignant was the fact when she met the bereaved family members they told her that my uncle had been remembering her the previous evening and was wishing that she would come. What pained my mother the most then, was the fact that she did not follow her instinct and meet her brother before he passed away. Despite what we all said to console her, this regret will stay with her.

All of us have similar stories; maybe they are not as sad, but often we all regret not acting upon the nudges of our subconscious. In most cases, our heart and gut are still our best guide and we best know truth by the way it feels.

Your mind has to navigate a labyrinth of spreadsheets, data and analysis to arrive at a decision and could get delayed. The heart has and will always know the way.

- 72 -

Travel Light, Travel Free

Disillusioned by the ways of the world a young man once went to a Zen master who sat meditating in repose. "The world is a maze to me" he said; "the more I try to figure it out the more confused and lost I feel". "What do you want from me?" asked the Zen master. The young man said "I seek clarity and joy. I want to be like you –free and peaceful"

The Zen master smiled. "Here", he said "I give you this magic bag. Carry it wherever you go and you will find what you are seeking". The young man thought this was simple enough. He saw the master holding the bag with ease but as soon as he took it from the master he was bent by the weight of the bag. He did not however, comment on it and quietly took the heavy bag and went on his way. As he continued on his journey the bag became a cumbersome load and he did not feel any closer to what he pursued. Tired and irritated he came back to the master. He removed the bag roughly from his back and tossed it in the direction of the master; "This bag is no magic" he said, however, even as he said this he noticed that the master picked up the bag lightly like it had no weight at all; while he could still feel the pain where the bag had dug into his back. He peered into the bag and found nothing.

"How come this empty bag feels so heavy to me?" he lamented. The Zen master smiled again. "Don't look inside the bag, look inside of you… for the weight lies there. The bag is just a representation. Anything in life will seem heavy if you carry a burden within you. Drop the regrets, the hurt, and the anger and see how light your bag becomes. Man is free the moment he wishes to be "

The young man realizes then that he was the impediment, the weight, the maze not anyone or anything else. He understood that when you prioritize personal freedom, let go of the shackles that weigh you down you are able to travel through life freely and in accordance with your heart.

73

Treasure Hunt

'Not all those who wander are lost, some are looking for garage sales'. I read this quote recently somewhere and it bought a smile to my lips as it is reminiscent of such carefree happy times.

My husband and I were then students at the University of Delaware in the USA. Come Saturday morning, we often found ourselves in our beat up Nissan Sentra, braced with maps scavenging for 'garage sales'. The entire concept really intrigued me. The paraphernalia of someone's home, someone's history, someone's childhood was literally out in the street and it could be yours for a very nominal price.

As students, cost was a huge factor in all we did, however, it was not just the financial aspect that drew us to these garage sales. Rummaging through objects that had become rather redundant for somebody but could be of value to someone else made these moments particularly affecting. Some of the most beautiful paintings I still have in my home, old records (Fleetwood Mac), wooden toys and some rare books came from garage sales. Just a pocket full of change could get you such treasures.

It was so much better than going to the malls. As the owner (sometimes reluctantly) sold the items he/she would tell us a little story behind each object. Each item then came with an antiquity that became a part of us when we brought it home. We heard stories of recalcitrant childhood, unwanted gifts from grandparents, dilemma of a newly married pair and the memories of a couple living in the same house for 50 years! Nostalgia, love, heartbreak, romance and wisdom permeated most of the stories we heard. Consequently, we didn't just buy the object we bought stories home as well.

Objects might lose some of their value over time, however, the emotions attached to them never quite fade away. Sometimes the best way to give permanency to objects that are no longer useful to you is by giving them away to someone else who needs them. Ernest Hemingway elucidates this notion so well in the flash fiction-a story in just 6 words. *"For sale: baby shoes, never worn."* Because of loss, the shoes could no longer have meaning for one couple but for someone else it could represent a whole new chapter in their lives.

Your disposition towards the things that belong to you is quite significant. If you develop a connection with the objects you own, you will treat them well. And once they have served their purpose for you, they will then be poised to do make life better for someone else.

74

Welcome to the Jungle

Life speaks to us in paradoxes, and we need to listen closely as it is these very absurdities that make the subsequent revelations more impactful.

A man troubled by the lack of fulfilment and meaning in his life seeks sense and tranquillity. His purpose seems unclear and life itself arbitrary. He goes to a sage seeking guidance. The sage speaks about karma and destiny. He further says that one should not fret petty things and keep going as the supreme God has a plan for everyone. When the man seeks clarity, the sage elucidates by presenting two scenes from a forest. In scene one an injured hungry hyena seems destined to die and in scene two a lion struggling with a wilful strong bull, finally goes for the kill. What connects these two scenes is the fact that once the lion had his fill he leaves the carcass to the injured hyena who had been lurking around the lion. The hyena survives.

The man is content by the sage's revelation. He rationalized that he struggled in vain. The mighty God who took care of the most fragile, pitiful and timid of his creations surely would take care of him too. Assuredly, God esteemed man above all his creations. Thus, he gave up on his strife and waited for benediction. He waited for his share to come to him automatically. He waited in vain, as it appeared that the Almighty had forgotten all about him. When he couldn't take it any longer he visited the sage again and demanded an explanation. The sage just smiled. "This is your journey" he equivocated. Disillusioned, the man called out to God asking him why his needs had been ignored when even a lowly beast like the hyena had been taken care of. At some point, he heard a voice:

It said "Yes, I do take care of my creation, but I created you a lion, not a hyena".

Sometimes your role and purpose in life seems elusive, illogical and hollow. It is in those times that you must remind yourself that the God who created the oceans, mountains and galaxies looked at you and thought: the world needs someone like you. You are exceptional with a unique destiny. Grab it by the horns.

75

What Goes Around Comes Around

The concept of karma underscores the fact that in the larger scheme of things, everything is connected and the good that we do might not have an immediate impact but at some point it will come back to us. We just need to patient and wait for the right dots to connect.

Now, if good deeds are rewarded, bad deeds are assuredly penalised. This is how the natural balance is restored. Karma has no deadline and here is a parable that underscores the fact that we cannot escape the consequences of our actions. A poor villager would carry a kilo of butter to a shop owner in the city. In exchange of which the shop owner would give him some sugar, salt and other essential items that the villager needed. This arrangement worked well as the shop owner got good quality butter and the poor villager was able to sustain his family by getting vital items for them. The shopkeeper however, being of a suspicious nature, decided to weigh the kilo of butter that the farmer got for him. To his shock he found that the butter actually weighed 900grams. This made him very upset and angry. When the farmer visited him next he pounced on him and demanded an explanation. The poor farmer joined his hands and explained, "Sir I am so poor I have no weights to weigh my provisions. On the scales I use, I usually put the one kg sugar you give me on one side and my butter on the other."

The shopkeeper had nothing left to say. His karma had caught up with him and let's just say he learnt his lesson.

We need to be a reflection of what we would like to receive. If you want love, give love. If you want the truth be truthful, if you want respect give respect. What you send out to the world… will return to you. Life is actually this simple. What complicates it is the fact that we anticipate more than what we deserve and forget that time is more powerful than all of us and that the Natural order will seek its balance.

After all, isn't our future is just an Echo of our past?

76

Where Dandelions Grow...

Irecently visited a friend who is a fervent gardener. She did have a lovely garden replete with exotic shrubs and plants. The lawn was well manicured and the bushes trimmed to perfection. It seemed not a petal was out of place. I almost touched the plants to see if they were real. However, despite the beauty and perfection I felt something was missing …everything seemed too perfect. Austere even.

During a stroll in this garden, my friend asked "So what do you think"? Always diplomatic, I told her I thought it was absolutely fantastic. "Perfect"! I repeated. She just smiled and we kept walking. It was then that I noticed a small patch of land that seemed unkempt somewhere in the margins of her beautifully landscaped garden. I all but ran towards it. There were lovely plants in that little garden, however they had not been sheared. There was nothing neat or tidy about this patch. The vines snaked with abandon. The bushes were frowzy. There were even weeds growing in there and no one seemed to care about it. It was such a striking contrast to what I had just witnessed. Confused, I asked my friend "What it this?"

She sagaciously answered-"This is where I let the dandelions grow."

I came to understand that our clinically conditioned lives need this patch of land where we are able to let go and let nature take its course. Instead of always pursuing order and control we could sometimes go with the flow and find imaginative new solutions to live life more dynamically. Alan Dean Foster the American writer says "Freedom is just chaos, with better lighting". Sometimes, however, just like the perfectly pruned plants, life can get too restrained, too plastic and this will not allow it to be meaningful and free. For example: Love brings in disorder and to love is to be vulnerable. Love anything, and your heart will certainly be wrung and possibly be broken. Love cannot be contained or clipped or fixed. We could avoid all entanglements; lock it up safe and tame it. But in that casket – safe, restrained, motionless, and airless – it will change. It will not be broken; it will become unbreakable, impenetrable, and irredeemable. The only place outside Heaven where you can be perfectly safe from all the confusions and perturbations of love is hell. So yes, love brings in weeds, brings in bedlam, but can you imagine a life without love?

By letting disorder reign in our life sometimes, or by not being disconcerted by it we could discover life's subtleties and avoid the traps of stereotypes. Beauty lies in surprises, in suspense and in waiting for life to reveal itself organically. It's time we realize our fractal connectedness to each other as we are all a part of the chaos that life generates. A good garden may have some weeds. Let them grow.

77

Well Done is Better Than Well Said

Time isn't precious at all, it is often the people we spent it with that makes time precious, and more often than not we realize this in retrospect. We recognize the essential points in our lives in remembrance, as we are too absorbed in the placid details of the present to understand what we are doing or where we are going. It is almost as though we navigate the present with our eyes blindfolded. Only when time removes this blindfold, we glance at the past and suddenly find that it is illuminated with meaning and wisdom.

Recently, I had to write a recommendation letter for a colleague with whom I had shared a relationship comprising of strong thoughts and emotions that swayed from one end of the spectrum to the other. All the time that we worked together the relationship was an emotional rollercoaster. We were good friends at times and at other times - rivals. The negativity was psychological as we never really explored the present or each other. The tug towards each other was always strong, however, disquiet and apprehension laced the moments we spent together.

Now, that our life had taken different directions, this act of writing the recommendation letter formed an axis mundi that dissolved the notion of past and present. The letter all but wrote itself; there were so many wonderful things that she had done and so many wonderful things that she had been that I smiled despite myself. As remembered all the laughter and promise, I wondered why our relationship had been so rocky.

It dawned on me then that in all our times together I had never once told her all the good things about her that I was now writing in this letter. I hadn't got around to telling her what a wonderful person she was. Although this letter would benefit her, we could never have our moment in time together. Life cannot be lived in retrospect. If there are good words to say, we must say them now; the present is the best time to do all of the things we've been wanting to do but have been putting off. If anything is worth doing, it's worth doing now.

After all, no matter how beautifully I write this letter, well done will always be better than well said.

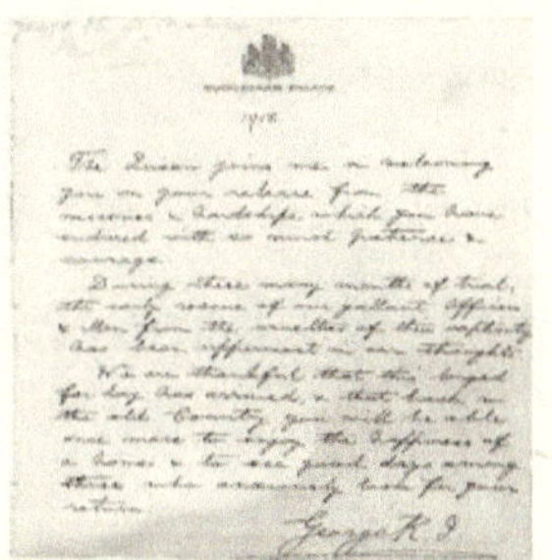

78

You Can Only Conquer Yourself

Recently, while doing a course, I was asked to do a simple yet interesting activity. I was given a list of things and had to deduce which of those things were well within my control, which I could influence but not really control and which were completely beyond my control. It seemed like a simple endeavor at first, however as I delved into the task I realized that there was not much I could control. At best I could attempt to influence a few things. While I was pondering over this exercise, a story I had heard a long time ago flashed in the mind's eye and suddenly the penny dropped.

A benevolent but rather foolish king disguised as a traveler roamed around his empire to gauge the principal problems his kingdom was facing. He walked around for days and was relieved to note that his people seemed happy. However, the rough terrain he walked on hurt his feet. Looking at his blistered toes the king got really annoyed. "I know what can make my land better" He said. "The landscape of my kingdom is very rough and it must be carpeted with rawhide immediately". While other courtiers speculated at how this mammoth feat could be achieved, the chief minister sat contemplative. He did not want to incur the wrath of the king by calling his idea ridiculous but at the same time could not ignore the wounds on the king's feet.

When the king finally prodded him he said, "What a wonderful idea Sire, however, I know how we could make this enterprise less expensive". The king was intrigued. The chief minister sagaciously continued "Instead of covering the entire kingdom in hide, why don't we cut two small pieces and cover your feet with them?" "What a wonderful idea!" the King exclaimed. Two pieces were quickly cut for the king and the rough terrain did not bother him anymore.

Wanting to influence the external is as futile and foolish as wanting to fix the terrain when it is your feet that are bothering you. Since there is precious little we can control, fixing or governing ourselves is not only simpler but the only viable option. Only when the inner landscape is flamed the whole world gets illuminated.

79

Zen on the Go

Life they say is full of paradoxes just like roses are full of thorns. This becomes only too apparent when I sit down to meditate, to quieten my mind, and it wanders in all possible directions. The more I try to reign it in the more it travels away from me. Disenchanted, I started looking for options to best govern my mind. I came across all kinds of tips and suggestions, however, none of them rang true. At last I came across a little anecdote that helped me gain some perspective.

A Zen student was particularly perturbed with his volatile nature. He felt his quick temper led him to situations that he could not control and kept him from gaining insight. He went to his master and sought his advice. To his amazement the master brushed him aside; "Come with a real problem" was all he said.

The young student was very disturbed by the master's reaction and could not fathom his apathy. He gathered some courage and went to him again. "Well" said the master then, "say you do have a peculiar malaise, let me see this volatile nature, this temper of yours."

Confused the student replied "I cannot just show it to you,"

"Then I'll wait till you can you show it to me" said the master.

"No point in waiting, it arises unexpectedly", said the student in dismay.

"Then it is not your true nature" said the master, "if it were, you would be able to show it to me here and now. Only your thoughts and reactions to those thoughts make it real. You have no temper. You never had. Let the thoughts of your temper come and go. Don't cling to them. Don't make them real"

After a moment of contemplation, the student laughed, suddenly enlightened.

I realized then that the reason one meditates is not to get rid of considerations but to become aware of them. Now when I meditate, I do let the thoughts navigate around me like the wind, however, I refuse to be swept away by them. Meditation consents that the mind goes in different directions, however, it also reminds us that, in any direction the mind travels unshackled, the sun will warm, the rain will cool and roses will bloom where it treads.

www.ingramcontent.com/pod-product-compliance
Lightning Source LLC
Chambersburg PA
CBHW032005050726
47590CB00006B/2052